The SPIRIT SPEAKS *the* GOSPELS

J Hiam

WESTBOW
P R E S S®
A DIVISION OF THOMAS NELSON
& ZONDERVAN

WestBow Press books may be ordered through booksellers or by contacting:

WestBow Press
A Division of Thomas Nelson & Zondervan
1663 Liberty Drive
Bloomington, IN 47403
www.westbowpress.com
844-714-3454

Scripture quotations marked NKJV are taken from the New King James Version.
Copyright © 1982 by Thomas Nelson, Inc. Used by permission. All rights reserved.

Scripture quotations marked CEV are from the Contemporary English Version
Copyright © 1991, 1992, 1995 by American Bible Society, Used by Permission.

ISBN: 978-1-6642-9544-5 (sc)
ISBN: 978-1-6642-9545-2 (e)

Library of Congress Control Number: 2023905024

Print information available on the last page.

WestBow Press rev. date: 06/23/2023

CONTENTS

PREFACE

God's will is the theme of this book. Through all opposition, the plan of God must be accomplished and followed, no mater the adversity and the pain of inadequate and ineffectual feelings.

President George Washington, who some say prayed five hours a day, is an example of doing the will of God; when he crossed the Delaware River on Christmas night, and marched on Trenton. All of his staff was telling him how he was "out of his mind" * and how it could not be done.

Our previous president, President Donald Trump, who said, "Jesus Christ was his boss," has suffered much humiliation and investigation, for six or seven years; because he is trying to help his fellow countryman and respect the call of God.

In writing this book the author of these writings, who has faced a number of issues, is very humbled to be a part of the voice of truth and has rejoiced in the depth of feeling and listening, when the Spirit Speaks.

Jesus Christ, the Son of God, the Holy Spirit, and the Father God, gives us the moral strength of the Trinity; to bring these writings forward to hear, when the Spirit Speaks.

J HIAM, author

*(As seen on Fox Nation, "The Crossing").

NOTES AND REFLECTION

"Fear God and give glory to Him…. worship Him, who made heaven And earth, the sea, and springs of water."
(Revelation 14:7)

....

....

....

....

....

....

....

....

....

....

....

....

....

....

....

....

....

THE GOSPELS

God's Plan

Then I saw another angel flying in the midst of heaven, having the everlasting gospel to preach to those who dwell on earth-to every nation, tribe, tongue and people (NKJV Revelation 14:6).

The Gospels bring the "good news" of Jesus' coming to earth. Jesus gives us a new heart, (Ezekiel 36:26) and God's Spirit, so we can have clean souls and pure thoughts; which was God's plan.

The four Gospels portray this in their teachings; characterized by four various perspectives from four different men of God. There were reasons why each wrote their books of the Gospels.

Matthew, writes for the Jewish people; helping them to understand Jesus and His teaching. They expected a warrior, like King David; who would save them from Roman dictators. They did not expect a Messiah of servitude and love; God's plan.

Mark wrote an action book to portray Jesus, to the Roman citizens, which helped identify God's plan.

Luke wanted to clarify any misunderstanding of God's plan.

John showed a personal relationship through the Holy Spirit, with the Son of God, which was God's plan.

All shared the truth and love of God's plan.

("Fear God and give glory to Him.... (NKJV Revelation 14:7).

Holy Spirit   Pray

    Action   The Gospels are known and loved by most truth-seeking people.

MATTHEW

Our King

"Behold, the virgin shall be with child, and bear a Son, and they shall call His name 'Immanuel' which is translated, "God with us" (NKJV Matthew 1:23).

In Matthew, Jesus is portrayed as royalty. He came as a king; the angels brought Him and stayed with Him until He left the earth. Matthew records Jesus' genealogy back to David and Abraham (Gen 12:3), and as a Jewish believer portrays Jesus as the Messiah. Jesus did not disappoint us.

Most of the Jewish leaders rejected Jesus as their Messiah and their Savoir. He came to us as the Son of God, to help people in their spiritual life; the Jews expected their Messiah to be a political figure, and save them from Rome.

Even today, people expect this from Jesus. Jesus is our God; our King!

("Go to the people of all nations and make them My disciples" (CEV Mt 28:19).

Holy Spirit Pray

    Action Let us show Christ, He is our King.

MATTHEW

Fulfillment of Scripture

Then Jesus asked them, "But who do you say I am." Peter Spoke up, "You are the Messiah, the Son of living the God" (CEV Matthew 16:15,16).

Matthew was a tax collector; Tax collectors kept records; he kept good records. The Bible gives us these detailed records in the Gospel of Matthew; it is the Gospel of fulfillment; portraying Jesus as the Messiah.

From this gospel comes the beatitudes of Jesus; He gives us moral law for His Kingdom; He speaks in parables; there are many miracles and healings done by Jesus. The two main commandments are given by Jesus, "Love the Lord with all your heart, soul, and mind; love others as we love ourselves (Mt 22:37).

(Jesus told His disciples not to tell anyone that He was the Messiah.) (CEV Mt 16:20).

Holy Spirit   Pray

Action   Let us show someone Jesus loves them; completely.

MARK

Serve

For even the Son of Man did not come to be served but to serve, and to give His life as a ransom for many (NKJV Mark 10:45).

Mark wrote for the Roman people; about 50% of which were slaves and servants. Mark in his writing of the Gospel pointed out Jesus' humbleness; His ability to be strong and help others understand the power from God.

He writes about Jesus' many miracles and His writings show God is with Jesus in His many healings and miracles; with the Holy Spirit guiding Him (Jesus) and with the power to rescue them from sickness, and death. Mark teaches how important it is to obey God and serve man.

(They said to Him, "We are able." So, Jesus said to them, "You will indeed drink the cup that I drink… (NKJV Mark10:39).

Holy Spirit   Pray

Action   Show Christ through our service to Him; we love and care for His people.

MARK

Savior of the World

"Yet it shall not be so among you; but whoever desires to become great among you shall be your servant (NKJV Mark 10:43).

In order to portray Jesus as someone most of the people in Rome could identify with, Mark wrote about Jesus' miracles and ability to heal the sick and lame. These people in Rome were doers; in our day they would make good business men.

Mark told about Jesus getting prepared to help others in his many tasks at hand. He wanted people of Rome to realize, faith in Jesus would not be easy. He prepared them, by teaching they should serve others, and keep God's Commandments.

Mark wanted to show that God, in anointing Jesus, and endorsing Him for His many tasks of healing and working miracles, presented Jesus as the Messiah and the world's Savior.

(Then a voice came from heaven, "You are My beloved Son, in whom I am well pleased" (NKJV Mark 1:11).

Holy Spirit Pray

    Action Our Savior did so much for us; let us show Him we appreciate Him and what He did for us.

LUKE

Humanity of Christ

Look at My hands and My feet and see who I am! Touch Me and find out for yourselves. Ghosts don't have flesh and bones as you see I have (CEV Luke 24:39).

In the Gospel, Luke is emphasizing that he is researching to find the truth of Christ. He writes for the Greeks, who were also preparing for the coming of Christ in their own way.

Luke points out that Jesus, came in human form to save man from his sins. He portrays the humanity of Christ; starting with Jesus at the age of twelve, getting lost from His parents and reminding His parent with the words, "Didn't you know I had to be in My Father's house?" Luke is the only Gospel that records this happening (Luke 2:49) about Christ's childhood; and the witness to Jesus' deity.

Christ is recorded to have started His ministry at the age of thirty and ended when He was thirty-three at the resurrection; which we experience today; through the Holy Spirit and our God, Jesus Christ who referred to Himself as the Son of Man.

(They gave Him a piece of baked fish. He took it and ate it as they watched.)

(CEV Luke 24:42,43)

Holy Spirit   Pray

Action   Jesus is our wonderful God; stay in His presence with prayer.

LUKE

Compassionate Man

They also say that all people of every nation must be told in My name to turn to God, in order to be forgiven (CEV Luke 24:47).

Even though Luke in his Gospel points out the characteristics of Jesus; He also gives us many happenings of the women in Jesus' life. He gives us the personal genealogy of Jesus through His mother Mary; which is traced back to Adam (the first man).

He gives us the Song of Mary; plus, Elizabeth, John the Baptist' mother. He shows us many compassionate situations such as; Mary Magdalene (Luke 8:2), Mary and Martha, Jesus' friends; many women He healed, women that followed Him to the cross and many after the resurrection.

Women were thought of as second-class citizens, when Jesus was on earth, which shows Jesus had a special compassion for all people.

(So, beginning in Jerusalem, you must tell everything that has happened.)

(Luke 24:48)

Holy Spirit   Pray

   Action   Thank God for Jesus' fairness toward all people. He is our amazing God. Unbelievable.

JOHN

The Word-Son of God

The Word became a human being and lived here with us. We saw His true glory. the glory of the only Son of the Father (CEV John 1:14).

John believed anyone who does not believe that Jesus is the Son of God is antichrist (1 John 2:22). Antichrist as we understand, have no conscience in keeping Jesus' teachings of Moral Law and God's Spoken word, which some would say makes these antichrists evil; they have no conscience against evil.

There are many ways that Jesus revealed He was the Son of God; His many miracles, many witnesses for Christ as the Son of God; Nathaniel, Peter, John the Baptist, and the list goes on and on.

Truth is what tells us Jesus is the Son of God: Jesus told us He would send us the Holy Spirit (Acts 2:2), He did; He would go to the cross, He did: He said He would rise in three days, He did; and the truth in our generation continues.

As Christians, we avowal through the Spirit of Truth; Jesus is and was the Son of God; not a prophet but the Son of God; making Jesus, God.

(From Him all the kindness and all the truth of God have come down to us.)

(CEV John 1:14)

Holy Spirit Pray

Action Love Jesus Christ with all your heart, soul, and mind; for caring for us.

JOHN

Personal Relationship

"For God so loved the world that He gave His only begotten Son, that whoever believes in Him should not perish but have everlasting life (NKJV John 3:16).

Jesus was not sent to the earth, so He could become the Son of God. In the beginning, He was the Son of God.

Jesus did not come to find fault with us, He came to teach us how to love God and to love each other; through His Moral Laws and God's Ten Commandments. He came to show us, God is love.

According to John, salvation is found through the believing and receiving of Jesus as the Son of God (John 1:12), and receiving the Holy Spirit; which gives us a personal relationship with Christ.

Salvation is not hereditary; we do not receive it through knowledge, through education or influence of man. It is not what we know but what we understand and are willing to follow. Jesus is the power and through His Holy Spirit, becomes our Savior.

(God did not send His Son into the world to condemn the world, but that the world through Him might be saved (NKJV John 3:17).

Holy Spirit Pray

Action Let us show we love Jesus 24/7; not just one hour a week. By doing this, we create a personal relationship with Christ.

ACTS

Holy Spirit Action

"But you shall receive power when the Holy Spirit has come upon you; and you shall be witnesses to Me in Jerusalem, and in all Judea and Samaria, and to the end of the earth (NKJV Acts 1:8).

Luke was a doctor, a gentile, and a Greek, who was believed to be helped by Paul with his conversion to Christ. He traveled with Paul extensively and made a detailed report of all the happenings (Acts) of the apostles through guidance of the Holy Spirit. This action was to show the life of Jesus after the resurrection, and ascension of Christ.

God's prophet (Jer 31:33) wrote that God would use the Holy Spirit for this purpose. We see this in action, in Acts, as it happens.

Even the coming of the Holy Spirit took a special event, and today, most Christians know about the Pentecost; when and how it happened, is read in Luke's detailed account of the events in the Book of Acts.

("Therefore, let it be known to you that the salvation of God has been sent to the Gentiles, and they will hear it!" (NKJV Acts 28:28).

Holy Spirit   Pray

Action   For what Christ has done for us, let us keep Him first in our lives.

ACTS

Acts Continuing

And they continued steadfastly in the apostles' doctrine and fellowship, in the breaking of bread and in prayers (NKJV Acts 2:42).

For Pentecost to happen and be reported with such strength in Acts, the Holy Spirit must be a high priority for God and His relationship with us; using the Holy Spirit to connect to our lives.

Jesus said, while He was here on the earth (Mt 12:31) that we should NEVER reject the Holy Spirit.

After Jesus' ascension, the Holy Spirit took over the apostles' lives, and Luke writes about the boldness and strength these apostles showed to the world.

Stephen was a prime example of this great testimony, (Acts 7) to Christ. Peter, Paul and many others were, also, involved all of their lives with Christ's teachings.

Acts in our life today is still continuing!

(Praising God and having favor with all the people. And the Lord added to the church daily those who were being saved (NKJV Acts 2:47).

Holy Spirit   Pray

   Action   It is a beautiful life to belong to Christ's church. He is an omnipotent God, who loves us.

Molded by Christ

And do not be conformed to this world but be transformed by the renewing of your mind, that you may prove what is that good and acceptable and perfect will of God (NKJV Romans 12:2).

In the pursuit of happiness, one needs to realize who is molding our lives. Our character and our attitude need to come from Christ through the Spirit. We like to think we are molding our own identity, but so often our parents, the 24/7 media, our culture and even our friends have a hand in our allowing them to take us down the wrong path from the righteous to the neutral. We are influenced by our environment, rather than the truth from within our soul.

We want to be a good Christian; we love and respect our God and His principles. It is very hard to follow our leaders' values, unless we stay in touch with His presence daily, by prayer and supplication; by doing so, we will stay passionate and righteous, for our Christ. Stand boldly!

(In Him was life, and the life was the light of men (NKJV John 1:4).

Holy Spirit Pray

Action Let us stay molded by Christ's teachings and God's word.

The Great Awakening

"God, who made the world and everything in it, since He is Lord of heaven and earth, does not dwell in temples made with hands" (NKJV Acts 17:24).

As we read about our Christian heritage in this country, we realize how important revivals are when coming back to Christ, happens; and has happened in our history.

This is not an overnight happening; this goes for years and sometimes decades, in the turning of attitudes and culture change; but it has been done. For example, the First Great Awakening started somewhere around 1730 and lasted until the 1770's. That means we would not have had the Declaration of Independence from Britain, had it not been for our Founding Fathers growing up during this great revival.

The Black Robed Regiment, as Britain named them, and blamed them would not have existed had it not been for George Whitefield* and some other strong men, who were employed by Christ. The men that signed the Declaration of Independence had grown up with these ministers in the culture of Christ. Is it any wonder that 34% of the Constitution was taken from the Bible.

God has a way of sending us a new generation of Godly people; just like He did for the Hebrew Nation before entering the Promise Land.

("Truly, these times of ignorance God over-looked, but now commands all men everywhere to repent (NKJV Acts 17: 30).

Holy Spirit   Pray

> **Action**   Let us realize, our country was created by God through our prayers.

*(Taken from The Building of the American Heritage, Rick Green and David Barton).

Civil Duty

"Whose image and inscription is this?" "Caesar's." and He said to them, "Render to Caesar the things that are Caesar's and to God the things that are God's."

(NKJV Matthew 22:20,21)

Jesus is not saying in this scripture, we should not get involved with our government. What He is saying is keep God first (Exodus 20:3) in our lives and in our relationships; then meet our civil duty.

In Jerusalem taxes had to be paid to Rome for their occupation of Israel; and the Hebrews resented it. Jesus is telling them how to meet the requirements of the laws of Rome and God.

In America, we too pay taxes for unfair laws, but we pay them as a duty to our country; taxes that go to abortion clinics, health care for others, sometimes costing $5,000, or more a year; with nothing in return. But, again, this is our duty as an American citizen; and also, to follow the law.

We must meet our civil duty, and get involved any way we can in our government. Jesus is telling us how we can do both at the same time.

(You shall not bow down to them nor serve them. For I, the Lord your God am a jealous God …. (NKJV Exodus 20:5).

Holy Spirit Pray

> **Action** "but showing mercy to thousands, to those who love Me and keep My commandments" (Exodus 20:6).

Loose Fence

"All day long I have stretched out My hands to a disobedient and contrary people" (NKJV Romans 10:21).

Our nice neighbor turns her head when people talk or say anything about God. She thinks everyone is so nice; her doctors are nice and very trustworthy; her neighbors are nice, friendly, and very kind; and her assistant has a very kind family, who said she would pray for her prior to surgery.

When going into surgery, one of the neighbors said to her, "God is with you." In front of the nurse, our nice neighbor seemed almost embarrassed by the remark. Her attitude seemed to be resentful and independent; boldness for God does not seem to go over well with her. Someone should tell her among all the nice, kind, trustworthy people, she is giving so much credit to, is the common denominator of Jesus' teachings and possibly Jesus Himself.

We will probably never know, if during all that pain, she came to God because of her need; but Jesus will.

("I was found by those who did not seek Me; I was made manifest to those who did not ask for Me" (NKJV Romans 10:20).

Holy Spirit   Pray

> **Action**   God is waiting for us to get off the loose fence and find Him. Find Christ and do not ever let go!

Arena of God

Till we come to the unity of the faith and of the knowledge of the Son of God… that we should no longer be children tossed to and fro and carried about with every wind of doctrine, by the trickery of men, in the cunning craftiness of deceitful plotting (NKJV Ephesians 4:13,14).

With the base of God, we can throw our children into the arena and let them think to learn.

Without Jesus' teachings and Jesus as their base, it is like being in an ocean, caught in the waves, to rough and overwhelming to handle. Not knowing where the waves are coming from and where they are leading.

Leaving woke behind, putting the Ten Commandments back on the wall, and possibly debating their meaning, truthfully, children like kindergartners would connect with these commandments. It gives them a base and a direction. Making them feel confident about themselves, because the commandments are easy to understand, and they are simple to follow; yet deep in nature or natural law.

The Ten Commandments are a Moral Law, that we all need!

(.. but, speaking the truth in love, may grow up in all things into Him who is the head---Christ (NKJV Ephesians 4:15).

Holy Spirit   Pray

Action   With Moral Law, we have not left them in the ocean. The Ten Commandments teaches the depth of natural law.

Moral Law

"Do not think that I came to destroy the Law or the Prophets, I did not come to destroy but to fulfill. For I say to you, that unless your righteousness exceeds the righteousness of the Scribes and Pharisees, you will by no means enter the kingdom of heaven" (NKJV Matthew 5: 17,20).

The Pharisees obeyed the laws for outward appearance, but did not let the laws change their hearts or their behavior.

Jesus said His followers needed more change of heart and soul. He said it is what God does inside of us, that takes us to heaven. We cannot change ourselves; we must be God centered not self-centered. We cannot depend on people's approval of us. We must depend, and be more reverent to God; going beyond keeping laws to understanding and loving the principles behind the law.

True Christianity is to obey the Ten Commandments and follow Jesus' character (New Testament) for Moral Law.

(......one jot or one tittle will by no means pass from the law till all is fulfilled.)

(NKJV Matthew 5: 18).

Holy Spirit   Pray

Action   Start or stay in a study group that is bible-based. This is a way to stay with Christ.

NOTES AND REFLECTION

"…that utterance may be given to me, that I may open my mouth
boldly to make known the mystery of the gospel…"
(Ephesians 6:19)

....
....
....
....
....
....
....
....
....
....
....
....
....
....
....
....
....
....

The Revival

To them God willed to make known what are the riches of the glory of this mystery among the Gentiles; which is Christ in you, the hope of glory. (NKJV Colossians 1:27)

All the men that wrote the Constitution, signed the Constitution, and fought for the Constitution, grew-up in the era of the revival; The Great Awakening. *

Some, as children would go to the tent meetings with many of the ministers, who were very involved with the awakening of the Christian belief. These ministers taught before and during 1730 to 1770, which was the Great Awakening.

What frames a revival? According to David Barton and Rick Green; we must ask God for a revival. Indicators of a revival are when individual and cultural changes begin. For example, people become interested in praying, going to church rather than to bars; the culture becomes ethical, and revivals bring moral clarity. If the culture does not change, it is not a revival. *

Since we are a microwave* country, we must realize, God does not move fast. He will send a new generation of believers in Christ; evil will disappear.

We must pray.

(As you therefore have received Christ Jesus the Lord, so walk in Him.)
(NKJV Colossians 2:6)

Holy Spirit   Pray

    Action   Revivals usually begin with us, and continues to a new generation.

*(Taken from, The Building of the American Heritage, Rick Green and David Barton).

Holy Spirit

For no other foundation can anyone lay than that which is laid which is Jesus Christ......Do you not know that you are the temple of God and that the Spirit of God dwells in you (NKJV 1 Corinthians 3:11,16).

Jesus is the foundation of our temple; the home of the Holy Spirit. All of us together are the house of God. So, this means you are the temple of the Holy Spirit (2 Cor 6:16), who is living within your soul.

God told us (Ezekiel 36:26), He would give us a new heart and a strong spirit; and He did; the second covenant. The Spirit of truth is what we depend on to follow Christ's teachings and His word; this gives us our conscience and our direction.

The Holy Spirit unites you with others in truth and love.

(.... for God's home is holy and clean, and you are that home.)
(LAB 1 Cor 3:17)

Holy Spirit Pray

   Action Thank God for such a wonderful plan. Do you find it great getting to know God?

Sacrifice

Then another of His disciples said to Him, "Lord, let me first go and bury my father." But Jesus said to him, "Follow Me, and let the dead bury their own dead." (NKJV Matthew 8:21,22)

Jesus did not hesitate to stand-up for His moral law. He stood for complete loyalty and obedience to His Father. This is what He expects from His followers. Obedience to God and Jesus should be a priority in daily walking with Christ.

When Jesus asked Peter the Apostle, to 'Feed His Sheep,' (John 21:17) Peter gave up a lot; time with his family, (he probably had children), his business (he was a fisherman), his way of life in general.

Sacrificially, nothing should stand in the way of following Christ.

Dr. Billy Graham is another example of self-sacrifice for Christ. He was taken away from his wife and four children many times. This was quite a sacrifice for all the family, to be sure, but he did it for God. God is first.

(Therefore, by Him let us continually offer the sacrifice of praise to God, that is, the fruit of our lips, giving thanks to His name (NKJV Hebrews 13:15).

Holy Spirit Pray

Action Working for Christ is so fulfilling and rewarding; in the end, the good outweighs the sacrifice.

Walking with the Spirit

Don't cause the Holy Spirit sorrow by the way you live…

(LAB Ephesian 4:30)

You grieve the Holy Spirit by not following Jesus' commands, and by your behavior not of God.

The Ten Commandments gives you the root to grow, as you should for Christ. This is the base for walking with God. Maturity of spirit is important in walking with Christ, and your walk with your fellowman.

We connect to God through the Holy Spirit, so you need to thank God for the Spirit in your soul, and stay in the presence of Jesus Christ.

The Holy Spirit and Jesus are both trying to protect us. So, you can understand, we have support when we experience sorrow or need, when we walk with Christ.

(….and be renewed in the spirit of your mind (NKJV Ephesian 4:23).

Holy Spirit   Pray

    Action   Stay with the Holy Spirit;
He keeps our footing sure.

Mind

Jesus said, "Love your God with all your heart, soul, and mind....
(The Life Application Bible Matthew 22:37)

In Deuteronomy, Moses uses the word might which means the strength of our physical and mental body. In Matthew, Jesus uses the word mind to finish this trio. He carries the meaning even farther; Behind this strength could be wisdom, understanding, intellect, reasoning, judgment, determination, and purpose to name just a few.

The Pharisees in having over 600 laws to prioritize from the most important to the lessor important, asked Jesus, to test and trap Him; which is the most important commandment? Jesus understood this and He assured them, using the Old Testament and the Ten Commandments; God's Word, to answer.

When standing for God as Jesus did, we have the Word of God as our source and base; It never fails us.

(.... I will put my spirit within you so that you will obey my laws and do whatever I command (LAB Ezek. 36:27).

Holy Spirit Pray

Action When getting to know God, we learn; There is power in the Word of God. We must learn to use it!

Heart

For a man's heart determines his speech, A good man's speech reveals his treasures within him. An evil hearted man is filled with venom, and his speech reveals it (LAB Matthew 12:34,35).

Jesus is telling us our hearts need to be clean and pure. The heart is the core and source of our speech. Basically, to clean up our speech, we need to let Jesus into our heart, and soul, and mind.

One of the fruits of the Holy Spirit is self-control. Self-control can be mastered with discipline, and the help of the Holy Spirit; a heart filled with Jesus.

(For by your words, you will be justified, and by your words, you will be condemned (NKJV Matthew 12:37).

Holy Spirit Pray

Action Good or evil; it is always your choice.
Jesus always gives us a choice.
Talk with Him today.

Self-Control

Dishonest money brings grief to all the family; but hating bribes brings happiness.

(Life Application Bible Proverbs 15:27)

Lack of control can leave a void to be taken up by selfish desires.

Jesus made a special place in our souls for Himself, and we have to be responsible for keeping that special place filled with HIs word; and prayer. If not these evil desires and coveting feelings come rushing in; then we are vulnerable to almost anything.

When we give up our faith nothing can keep the evil away. Evil will be in control; evil cannot be fought alone. One of the fruits of the Spirit is self-control; A Gift!

(… not greedy for money. But hospitable, a lover of what is good, sober-minded, just, holy, self-control (NKJV Titus 1:7,8).

Holy Spirit   Pray

Action   Thank God for His requirement of obedience.

The Covenants

...those who teach God's laws and obey them shall be great in the Kingdom of Heaven (Life Application Bible Matthew 5:19).

This tells us The Ten Commandments are still extremely important to follow and obey; The principles behind the law of God's truth.

Even though the Ten Commandments were the first covenant of God's plan; Jesus and the Holy Spirit are the second covenant. Both are important, Jesus ranking the highest; because He is the understanding and discernment behind the truth. Both are Moral Law.

(....... loaded down with sins...always learning and never able to come to the knowledge of the truth (NKJV 2 Timothy 3:7).

Holy Spirit Pray

> **Action** Make a commitment to follow and obey both covenants as closely as possible; it is for our own good.

Black Robed Regiment

Be sober, be vigilant, because your adversary the devil walks about like a roaring lion, seeking whom he may devour (NKJV 1 Peter 5 8).

According to the United Kingdom in 1776, we would not have had a revolution had it not been for what they called 'The Black Robed Regiment' in America.

The Black Robed Regiment, were ministers of America who were involved with the Great Awakening of Jesus Christ; like all the Founding Fathers of that era. They put on their black robes, gave their sermons; took off their robes, grabbed their guns and fought the British. Our ministers today could keep better control of the people with this kind of inspiration, the media has control of our people; which the media knows it does. Is this our problem in America today; division?

God first! We are united through the Spirit. God is everywhere, including our politics and our government; that is where our ministers and Christians need to be. We are the government!

(You shall have no other gods before Me. You shall not bow down to them nor serve them (NKJV Exodus 20:3,5).

Holy Spirit Pray

Action Are we bowing down to our desired media, and our political party; or are we serving our God and keeping Him first with truth, forgiveness and caring of any political party or race? Read American documents; Declaration of Independence, Constitution, Bill of Rights, with the books that go with them, and the list goes on; we cannot keep God first in our government without this knowledge of documents and truthful history.

Fear Walls

There is no fear in love; but perfect love casts out fear, because fear involves torment. But he who fears has not been made perfect in love.
(NKJV 1 John 4:18)

As a child, a great number of us got criticized by a prejudice feeling adult; many times, unfairly. Even though, we may have been innocent of the deed, we were still in the way of someone's anger and frustration; and we scaldingly carry the burden and blame for something we did or did not do.

So often, in defense, we build-up invisible walls. With these fear walls, we go through life not finishing the job God has given us to do. It is not whether we are right or wrong, after the job is accomplished, it is the fear of prejudice criticism, we have a hard time facing. Praying our way through these invisible walls and tearing them down, is our job as a praying minute-by-minute Christian. We have to work at accomplishing this, and growing with the Spirit of Christ. Growing and learning, always gets better, when we know we will meet Him on the other side of our walls.

(We love Him because He first loved us (NKJV 1 John 4:19).

Holy Spirit   Pray

Action   Even better, we know He is with us while walking through our fear walls. He loves us very much!

Trust

The Lord gives perfect peace to those whose faith is firm. So, always trust the Lord because He is forever our mighty rock (CEV Isaiah 26:3,4).

As we get to know the Lord, we find He gives love, joy and peace to us through the Holy Spirit.

We go through the world of chaos and problems daily. It is like going to our own special island when we turn to our Lord, and find such feelings of peace and joy. In getting to know God, we learn trusting Him, in order to work with Him and grow our faith in Him, is paramount in our relationship with Him.

(Guard what was committed to your trust, avoiding the profane and idle babblings and contradictions of what is falsely called knowledge).

(NKJV 1 Timothy 6:20).

Holy Spirit Pray

    Action We need to Honor our Lord by keeping His word (truth). Jesus is so trustworthy; It is not hard to trust Him.

The Cover-up

Note those who cause divisions and offenses… For those who are such do not serve our Lord Jesus Christ, but their own belly, and by smooth words and flattering speech deceive the hearts of the simple (NKJV Romans 16:17,18).

Something "unprecedented" has happened in our country. Our Previous President, who is the best president in our history for honesty, integrity and constitutionally getting things accomplished, has just had his home raided, by the questionable F.B.I. This Previous President is such a righteous person, handpicked by God, has never had as much as a traffic ticket. While watching television, we realize the oval office is overreaching the Constitution 2.1.8, 2.3.1.

Is this another setup by our evil corrupt government: did they find (fake) papers showing our Previous President in an evil light; did they find (fake) proof, this Previous President is to overthrow our government. Will their scheme work?

Our former president and his colleagues, who are working in the People's White House, said that this is not a Christian nation; this is a Muslim nation; now we can believe him. Is the FBI trying to protect someone by this action? Why try to divert our attention? What truth in reality is being covered-up?

(… but I want you to be wise in what is good, and simple concerning evil. And the God of peace will crush Satan under your feet shortly (NKJV Romans 16:19,20).

Holy Spirit   Pray

> **Action**   If they are successful, we will lose our country, and our Constitution. Hold on to your guns and pray, just like we have been doing since 911; our former president and his colleagues said so; they are noticing!
> With all your heart, soul, and mind pray and STAY WITH CHRIST!

A Higher Source

… That you, being rooted and grounded in love, may be able to comprehend with all the saints what is the width and length and depth and height--- to know the love of Christ (NKJV Ephesians 3:17,18,19).

When we start thinking of our country and our culture, we realize our standards are very low; we ask what is needed to correct this problem? For example, America was #1 with literacy, which changed after 1960, when they took God out of our Schools. Compared to other countries, we now rank 65, or less.

Are we teaching our children, how to relate to a higher source or standard? Are we giving them stretch goals, which teach them to think on their own and find the true God? When we give up God, we, in our learning go horizonal, instead of vertical in the thinking process.

God is omnipotent. We will never reach Him totally, but we can learn and teach our children how to think widely to touch the stars; how to think deeply to find our God.

(…which passes knowledge; that you may be filled with all the fullness of God.)

(NKJV Ephesians 3:19b)

Holy Spirit Pray

    Action We need to fly with God, rather than be molded to a nest. It is wise to stay with God; never let go.

God's Boundaries

For no sooner has the sun risen with a burning heat than it withers the grass; its flower falls and its beautiful appearance perishes. So, the rich man also will fade away in his pursuits (NKJV James 1: 11).

A man who worships tangible or intangible assets is like a flower that will soon lose its beauty; fade and wither; killed by the summer sun.

When we focus on ourselves rather than on God we are moving out of God's boundaries and into our selfish thoughts and attitudes. We should find our treasures of life not through tangible assets, but growing spiritually, physically, and mentally through the process of prayer and staying close to God.

(Who would form a god or mold an image that profits him nothing?)
(NKJV Isaiah 44:10)

Holy Spirit   Pray

Action   Let us ask ourselves: "Whom do I Trust?
"Where do I look for Truth?
"Where do I find my security?
(Life Application Bible, page 1031)

Co-workers

Apollos and I are working as a team, with the same aim… We are only God's co-workers. And no one can ever lay any other real foundation than that one we already have – Jesus Christ. Then every workman who has built on the foundation with the right materials and whose work still stands, will get his pay.

(The Life Application Bible 1 Corinthians 3:8,9,11,14)

Paul and Apollos' aim of course is to build on the foundation that which Jesus had already laid. They seem to have done a great job working for the good of Christ.

Jesus does not pick just anyone; He picks the best character. That means Paul and Apollos would have had already great integrity and very high moral standards before Christ chose them. Someone who can understand how to get the job done.

(For we are God's fellow workers…… (NKJV 1 Corinthians 3:9).

Holy Spirit   Pray

Action   Pray for your co-workers.
Learn to love like Jesus loves.

God Omniscient

For You formed my inward parts; You covered me in my mother's womb. I will praise You, for I am fearfully and wonderfully made; marvelous are Your works, and that my soul knows very well. My frame was not hidden from You, When I was made in secret, and skillfully wrought in the lowest parts of the earth.

(NKJV Psalm 139:13,14,15)

This verse says it all; how omnipotent is our God?

God's character shows, He is a very loving and understanding God; we have a very forgiving God; He does not condemn mistakes; He may not like how mistakes are handled, but He is there for us.

Mistakes are one thing; evil is something else. That is your choice. Do not listen to deceitful lies. He knows all; He is all-seeing and all-knowing. Follow Christ's path, meaning do His will; His way. He will take care of us; He is omniscient.

(You saw me before I was born and scheduled each day of my life before I began to breathe. Every day was recorded in your book (LAB Psalm 139:16).

Holy Spirit   Pray

   Action   Christ has given us the choice of trial. Trust Him.

Ransomed from Hell

I bless the holy name of God with all my heart. Yes, I will bless the Lord and not forget the glorious things He does for Me. He forgives all my sins, He heals me. He ransoms me from hell (LAB Psalm103:1,2,3,4)

Getting to know God can be both exciting and personal. To be able to feel the Holy Spirit in our soul is completely awesome. To know this experience comes from Jesus Christ personally; it is inspiring. He gives justice to all who are treated unfairly; He reveals His will to us; He is slow to get angry and He loves with an everlasting love. He is constantly with us.

He has mighty angels listening and carrying out His every command, who serve Him constantly. These are just some of the characteristics of the Father God and His Son Jesus the Christ.

(How precious it is Lord, to realize you are thinking about me, constantly.)

(LAB Psalm139:17)

Holy Spirit   Pray

Action   Learn to Trust God; read the Bible every day; Pray.

NOTES AND REFLECTION

"For your Father knows the things you have
need of before you ask Him."
(Matthew 6:8)

....

....

....

....

....

....

....

....

....

....

....

....

....

....

....

....

....

THE LORD'S PRAYER*

Our Father which art in heaven, (v9)

In the Old Testament, many feared to speak God's name for fear of offending Him. Everything Christ did during His last three years of His life, He did for Our Father, and humanity. During this time people regarded God as someone in heaven too high to relate strong feelings toward. Not only did Jesus bring us truth and grace, but He also introduced us to a beautiful Father who loves us very much. Jesus' Father loves us; He sent His Son to die for us; to save us from evil, and help to understand Him better.

Jesus was very successful with communication between humanity, and our loving God. Jesus achieved all.

(…pray to your Father who is in the secret place; and your Father who sees in secret will reward you openly" NKJV Matthew 6:6).

Holy Spirit Pray

Action Jesus' words of "Our Father", give us a closeness to God that we need in our communication with God, in prayer. He helped us to understand the Father; and He still does.

*(Taken from The Holy Bible, King James Version, ST. Matthew 6:9-13).

THE LORD'S PRAY

Hallowed be thy name. (v9)

Jesus' total respect for God is very clear in the Bible. He points out God's attributes in everything He (Jesus) does; and everything He does, He does it for the One who sent Him.

The Lord's Prayer is no different; He teaches us God's name is sacred; God is Holy, and is to be communicated with through the recognition of total respect.

We must never try to domesticate God. To use Him for our own selfish agenda would be considered idolatry.

Falling in love with God is easy to do, once we learn to know Him. Staying in love with Him is what Jesus is teaching us to do through prayer.

(You shall be holy for I; the Lord your God am holy (NKJV Lev 19:2).

Holy Spirit   Pray

> **Action**   God is within our reach now, because of what Jesus did for us; on the cross. Jesus did it all!

THE LORD'S PRAYER

Thy Kingdom come. (v10)

Jesus is teaching the Kingdom is coming and it is near (Luke 21:31).

Many of Jesus' followers had a hard time understanding what He meant when He said, "Repent, for the Kingdom of Heaven is at hand" (Mt 4:17). Even though Jesus Himself told us, "…the Kingdom of God is within you (Luke17:20).

Franciscan Priest Richard Rohr, says, "The Kingdom is the Really Real." * This means when we have gotten rid of our quilt and shame from our soul; then face the truth, God's truth; It is the Really Real coming through our soul. We must pray for our true self. This is just a taste of what we will experience in the Kingdom of Heaven.

("Assuredly, I say to you this generation will by no means pass away till all things take place" (Luke 21:32).

Holy Spirit Pray

> **Action** Let us pray to keep a clean and pure soul for God's Kingdom to live within us.

*(Taken from the Book, "Jesus' Plan for a New World, The Sermon on the Mount," by Richard Roher, with John Feister).

THE LORD'S PRAYER

*Thy will be done in earth, as
it is in heaven. (v10)*

Being humble with prayer, puts us on the path to doing God's will.
A lot of discernment and understanding, after reading God's word,
will also keep us on that path of righteousness.

Being independent from God by doing our own thing, brings about
arrogance and pride; which puts us on the path of self-destruction
and fighting evil alone.

God knows all of this; He must demand His will be done for our
protection; for our own good. God's will is to keep our souls pure
and holy at all times, then the Holy Spirit can do His work; growing
in spirit until we are ready to take the next step and that next step
will be between you, God and the Holy Spirit.

("For I have come down from heaven, not to do My own will, but the
will of Him who sent Me" (NKJV John 6:38).

Holy Spirit Pray

Action Finding God's will, is sometimes very hard to do, but
if we persevere; pray, staying close to God and Jesus
through the Holy Spirit; we will find the answers;
sometimes quickly and sometimes it takes a while; in
God's time, it is the right time.

THE LORD'S PRAYER

Give us this day our daily bread. (v11)

God is the living God. He works in our lives to give us both nourishment for our bodies and spiritual nourishment for our craving soul. James tells us "Every good gift and every perfect gift is from above (James 1:17), and comes down from the Father of lights. So, whatever is needed for the bearing of our food comes from God.

Jesus says to seek God first, and the rest will be added as needed (Mt 6:35). He kept God first; and He was referencing Himself as the bread (John 6:33) from heaven. We must ask for the spiritual bread that Jesus is talking about; it is our bread for daily prayer, meditation, and communicating with the Holy Spirit. This brings about changes in our lives, to transform ourselves and others into people who are serious about God's purpose, and His will.

It is said, "We are what we eat"; both physically, mentally, and spiritually.

("I am the living Bread which comes down from heaven. If anyone eats of this bread he will live forever; and the bread that I shall give is My flesh, which I shall give for the life of the world" (NKJV John 6:51).

Holy Spirit   Pray

    Action   Falling in love with Christ makes us realize, after eating His bread, we will live forever. Let us eat Jesus' bread always.

THE LORD'S PRAYER

And forgive us our sins, (v12)

We cannot have a self-satisfying soul; therefore, it is so important to find God's truth. When we do not feel convicted of our sin, how are we to relate to God? Do we ignore our sin – thinking we are innocent? Do we humbly ask God to show us our sin, so, we can face truth and ask for forgiveness? The latter sounds like we are on the correct path.

Many will not face or want to be responsible for what they are doing or have done. His statement of "Forgive us for our sin," leaves the door open for the Holy Spirit to convict us of our sin and then, we can face the responsibility for the sin.

After dealing with it, and presenting it to Jesus for forgiveness, we can be assured we have been forgiven. Grace from our God is so important; it keeps us growing spiritually; and in the end it can even make us physically healthy.

(In whom we have redemption through His blood, the forgiveness of sins.)

(NKJV Col 1:14)

Holy Spirit Pray

Action Jesus makes it so easy for us to love Him.

THE LORD'S PRAYER

As we forgive those who sin against us. (v12)

There are different types of relationships that we encounter daily. We create even more as we go on our journey of life.

So, it means we must work at knowing our real feelings and dealing with these inner feelings. This is not hard to do, when we start realizing what Jesus suffered for us on the cross. He was humble, even to the point of washing the Disciples' feet. He hung on a cross; naked.

He is the Son of God; He did not have to do this! Why did He?

Leaving reconciliation aside, Jesus knew in our heart, we can hold no grudges or resentments toward our colleagues and still stay in the grace of God. He wants our heart, soul, and mind, to be pure from negative feelings. Then, we will grow in trust and love, humbly; for our God, our fellowman, and ourselves.

(If we confess our sins, He is faithful and just to forgive us our sins and to cleanse us from all unrighteousness (NKJV 1 John 1:9).

Holy Spirit Pray

Action Forgiveness is extremely important as a follower of Christ; He talked about this all the time. We must keep our soul clean and learn to love; Jesus shows us how to do this. He is an excellent Leader!

THE LORD'S PRAYER

And lead us not into temptation, (v13)

We have said before, we cannot fight evil alone. This is true also of sin and temptation. Freedom means freedom of choice between good and evil.

Do not blame God when we are tempted; God cannot be tempted (James 1:13) by evil. Therefore, He does not tempt us with evil intent. The evil comes from within our own soul; possibly from an evil spirit. So, when Jesus says, "lead us not into temptation;" He means do not let us let go of God, that we can be tempted; so, we do not give in to the evil desires of sin. God will always help us out of temptation and sin; if we ask Him, as Jesus is telling us to do.

God is not a dictator; we must humbly pray and ask.

(...the Father who created all the lights in the heavens. He is always the same and never makes dark shadows by changing (CEV James 1:17,18).

Holy Spirit Pray

    Action Do research on the Lord's Prayer, Jesus is giving us. Understanding God is very important in life.

THE LORD'S PRAYER

But deliver us from evil. (v13)

God is not a dictator. He trusts us to make our own choices, between good and evil. The problem is, we as humans are very vulnerable to evil; and are we responsible enough to see the correct choice? We must ask God even before we make these decisions. If not, it may lead to sin or even to evil. The Holy Spirit is there for us 24/7; He expects us to ask. Let us humble ourselves and ask.

This is another petition that stimulates our soul and makes us stronger when we realize, in truth, we are God's children.

This means God loves us, and we love Him for it. He will deliver us from evil. But we must respectfully ask!

(And the Lord will deliver me from every evil work and preserve me for His heavenly kingdom. To Him be glory forever and ever. Amen!)
(NKJV 2 Tim 4:18)

Holy Spirit   Pray

   Action   God loves us so much; He sent His Son to help us and give us grace.

THE LORD'S PRAYER

Benediction

For Thine is the Kingdom and the Power and the Glory forever. Amen!

The Benediction of Jesus' Prayer is important to finish a beautiful prayer of such meaning, and necessary for the understanding of God.

Jesus is telling us through the prayer, what is important to God and His relationship to us.

All through the Bible, we are encouraged by the writers to always honor and respect God. Praise from His people are important to Him. Our reverent praise of His attributes is how He responds to our petitions, and prayers to Him. It opens the door to communication between God and man. It is imperative to choose Him freely, and come to Him with our petitions, our praise, and our gratitude.

God's Glory is love from His people, and in return He pours out His character, His gifts, His rewards, and His love for us; through Jesus Christ.

(This is the day the Lord has made; we will rejoice and be glad in it.)
(NKJV Psalm 118:24)

Holy Spirit Pray

  Action We, as followers of Christ, need to do research on the Lord's Prayer. Jesus thought it important in order to know God.

Shame

....and when they had called for the apostles and beaten them, they commanded that they should not speak in the name of Jesus, and let them go. So, they departed from the presence of the council, rejoicing that they were counted worthy to suffer shame for His name (NKJV Acts 5:40,41).

They thought in Jesus' day, shame for Jesus' cause of witnessing, was an honor and a blessing. The apostles were very committed to Jesus, and to the cause of spreading the word of God to whomever and wherever. They had seen so much; it would be almost impossible not to know the truth of Christ; and not to have faith in God and His Son.

It must have been quite an exciting experience to get a new loving heart and have the Holy Spirit in their soul. It is even today!

(...they did not cease teaching and preaching Jesus as the Christ (NKJV Acts 5:42).

Holy Spirit   Pray

   Action   Say Jesus' name ten times out loud to someone.

Abundance

I have come that they may have life, and that they may have it more abundantly.

(NKJV John10:10)

The key to crossing the bridge between belief and experience is obedience. *

He opens your eyes to truth as you learn to trust Him, and obey His principles. This is the exciting part of learning and having an intimate relationship with the Lord. As your feelings grow, and you listen to His word; He in turn will bless you. He will take you out of your comfort zone, and put you into a moment-by-moment relationship with Him; growing and maturing in spiritual faith and purity.

As your character develops, and caring for Him gets stronger; you will not only want to do His will, but will start helping Him help others; to see this wonderful experience of life.

(... Though He was a Son, yet He learned obedience by the things which He suffered (NKJV Hebrews 5:8).

Holy Spirit   Pray

>   **Action**   Obedience to God and His word is a must; for your sake.

*(Taken from Dr. Charles Stanley, Life Principles Bible)

Temple of the Holy Spirit

Do you not know that you are the temple of God and that the Spirit of God dwells in you? If anyone defiles the temple of God; God will destroy him. For the temple of God is holy, which temple you are (NKJV 1 Corinthians 3: 16,17).

Our bodies are the temple of the Holy Spirit. God promised us a new spirit and He kept His word; the name Immanuel means 'God with us;' in the temple. This means that when we gather, we are the house of God. It is important to always keep our bodies and our souls pure and holy. We cannot have friction, division, controversy, resentment, or other sins as members come together to worship God.

The Trinity of God the Father, Jesus Christ the Son, and the Holy Spirit is always with us.

(Jesus answered and said to them," Destroy this temple and in three days I will raise it up" (NKJV John 2:19).

Holy Spirit   Pray

Action   We should feel honored to have such an amazing God. Stay with Christ; we are blessed!

Scapegoating

He then would have had to suffer often since the foundation of the world; but now once at the end of the ages. He has appeared to put away sin by the sacrifice of Himself (NKJV Hebrews 9:26).

The Jewish people would sacrifice two goats; the first goat was confessed over and killed; hoping to kill the people's sin. Confessions of sins were made over the head of a live second goat, and on the Day of Atonement, the people would "far remove" this goat to the desert; hoping the sins would be carried to another country.

Today scapegoating is a way for the dishonest media to entice people to watch their program. Mostly on the left of the political aisle. They have used former presidents on the opposite side, skin color, 17-year-old boys, any one on the opposite side of the aisle, and the list goes on. This lying, scapegoating, money-making scheme, empowers the people, who are thirsty for this kind of gossipy reckoning; it is almost evil. They are living in a bubble of ignorance.

Jesus was symbolic for the first goat; He died away our sin; He was the lamb of God. With the second goat, we do not have to scapegoat other people. All we must do is talk and tell our sin to Christ. Live for Christ; not gossip.

(….. so, Christ was offered once to bear the sins of many, He will appear a second time …...for salvation (NKJV Hebrews 9:28).

Holy Spirit   Pray

> **Action**   Do not be taken in by scapegoaters; look for truth. We depend on truth to save our country; it is everyone's responsibility.

Ignorant Division

"Woe to you, scribes and Pharisees, hypocrites! For you travel land and sea to win one proselyte, and when he is won, you make him twice as much a son of hell as yourselves (NKJV Matthew 23:15).

As Christ's Followers, God is our base; God comes first! From our base comes levers of love, trust, support, discernment, understanding, and the list goes on. But to deal with the world, we must pursue truth first.

Many in the news media do not meet these criteria levers; as a daily watch on television. It is very important to understand that God's people of integrity and truth, do not choose the media controlling fictional spin. If we are God's people, we embrace truthful media and truth filled politicians. We cannot allow ourselves to be misled by a narrative controlling and bottom-line profit media.

Instead of division, if we can find common ground by truth, we can learn to fight again together from both sides of the debate and we can win, for America.

("For you shut up the kingdom of heaven against men; for you neither go in yourselves, nor do you allow those who are entering to go in.)
(NKJV Matthew 23:13)

Holy Spirit Pray

Action Jesus faced the same problem in Israel as He does in America. Be kind to God; He is kind to you! FACE truth.

Duty to Government

"Sir, we know you are very honest and teach the truth regardless of the consequences, without fear or favor. Now tell us, is it right to pay taxes to the Roman government or not? (LAB Matthew 22:16,17)

Jesus was wise and knowledgeable about God's way. He is telling us to submit to the laws of the government. Show respect to the laws of our government as we show respect to the laws of God (2 Peter 2:13).

An example of this would be the Roe vs Wade law that was made in the 70's. Most all Christians submitted to civil duty, even though it was against our spiritual beliefs. Our government, also, made us pay taxes to abortion clinics and agencies of pro-abortion. These tax laws should change, now that this law of Roe vs Wade has been struck down; and through our Constitution, we will have a democratic way of handling this controversial problem, state by state.

This shows us, we must stay involved with our government; practicing our spiritual beliefs, with our civil duty, as an American citizen; * keeping God first and at the helm.

(Honor all people. Love the brotherhood, Fear God, Honor the King.)

(NKJV 1 Peter 2:17)

Holy Spirit Pray

>   **Action** Our country needs us. Memorize the Constitution. Stay with Christ.

*(Taken from Constitution Alive, David Barton and Rick Green).

Submission to Christ

Say to God, "How awesome are your works!" Through the greatness of Your power Your enemies shall submit themselves to You (NKJV Psalm 66:3).

Our borders have been open for well over a year, with millions hitting our shores. We ask ourselves, why would a man who did not want his kids in a 'racial jungle,' create a 'racial jungle'?

Hundreds of years ago, Turkey was taken over, as well as Spain; Italy's Mafia was created and used as their defense; France and England learned to climb trees.

The bones are not together yet; what is possibly the plan; a gun grab, the elderly sugar daddy to pass on, the bomb to find its direction, or a longer peaceable settlement.

If we hope to save America, and our way of life with the Constitution, we must realize, we cannot save it without submission to our King; Jesus Christ.

(… and that every tongue should confess that Jesus Christ is Lord, to the glory of God the Father (NKJV Philippians 2:10).

Holy Spirit   Pray

Action   Always, first-things-first. Show Christ, we love Him, just as He loves us. We must never take the attitude; we can go it alone;
The pendulum swings!

NOTES AND REFLECTION

JESUS OF NAZARETH,
THE KING OF THE JEWS.
(John 19:19)

The Resurrection

So, when the centurion and those with him....... feared greatly, saying, "Truly this was the Son of God!" (NKJV Matthew 27:54)

Some say they do not believe in the resurrection, because they do not believe God would be that cruel to His own Son. All the disciples were afraid, until they saw that Jesus had risen from the dead; just as He said He would. Almost all the apostles led a bold and fearless life and died like Jesus; a martyred death.

God did not baby His Son, and He does not baby us!

Jesus came to the earth to sanctify His people in God, and the resurrection did that for us. In the beginning of Christ's ministry (John 1:29), even John the Baptist called Jesus, the lamb of God.

People forget, we do not take our bodies with us; we probably get new unlimited bodies called, heavenly bodies. So, God is not a cruel God. God is a just and fair God; who has shown He loves us, and He probably loves and respects His Son even more.

(Then the angel spoke to the women.... "Go quickly, and tell His disciples that He has risen from the dead" (LAB Matthew 28:7).

Holy Spirit Pray

Action In Sanctifying us in God, we do not have to carry guilt of sin; we ask for forgiveness to purify our soul (Jere 31:34), and then we are free to humbly grow and mature in spirit. This is what Jesus did for us, by going to the cross.

A Friend

My help comes from the Lord, who made heaven and earth. He will not allow your foot to be moved; He who keeps you will not slumber. The Lord is your keeper; The Lord is your shade at your right hand. The Lord shall preserve you from all evil; He shall preserve your soul (NKJV Psalm 121:2,3,5,7).

Jesus seems to know how to expose evil and evil partakers. He understands how to deal with the Evil One and his bad angels; with a snap of His finger, they are gone, Awesome!

The problem is, how does He, God, wake up humanity to the realization of these serious events; independence of God is NOT Awesome!

But on the bright side, isn't it fantastic that we can have such a person to be by our side? Totally independent people are not wise, when they give away such an opportunity; To have such a friend, is an honor. As followers of Jesus, we can just taste the beauty of it all; Awesome!

("No longer do I call you servants...but I have called you friends....")
(John 15:15 NKJV)

Holy Spirit   Pray

Action   "You are My friends if you do whatever I command you." (For your protection.) (John 15:14 NKNV)

Jesus Calls

Then He added, "Now go away and learn the meaning of this verse of scripture, "It isn't your sacrifices and your gifts I want—I want you to be merciful.'

(The Life Application Bible Matt 9:13a)

We read and accept Matthew in the Bible, but 2,000 years ago Matthew, in the Jewish culture and in their minds of acceptability and appropriation was a porn star; a morally dirty tax collector, who was called by Jesus.

Today, Joshua, a very celebrated, award winning, sick to his stomach man was a porn star living a life in the porn business. People committing suicide because, not only were they rejected by their friends, their families and society, they rejected themselves every day. Joshua, on Tucker Carlson Today, said he left everyone and everything behind for money; trying to live in a world of total sin.* We will never really know how this young man felt every day; feeling alone, empty, and useless; living in a power-driven sex world and sex trafficking; living as a prostitute openly on camera, with thousands watching him perform. With this kind of degradation, it is hard to survive. His face was splashed all over the internet, there was no way out! Then, Jesus called him!

Jesus forgives us for our sins, but like Joshua said being responsible for our sin, the transition is hardly survivable. Joshua today is married, has three boys and is working for Christ as a preacher. He is also, working to get laws passed, so this filthy business will be, at least, limited as to what can be done in our society.

("For I have come to urge sinners, not the self-righteousness, back to God.")

Holy Spirit   Pray (LAB Matt 9:13b)

Action   Thank You God, for being such a great forgiving God!

*(Taken from Tucker Carlson Today, Fox Nation.)

A Brother of the Prodigal Son

"But as soon as this son of yours came, who had devoured your livelihood with harlots, you killed the fatted calf for him" (NKJV Luke 15:30).

It is hard for us as every day Christians to accept this kind of behavior. There are so many questions in our mind and in our attitude. As a Follower of Christ, we must accept and forgive these behaviors. After we feel personally our morals are being shaken, and our attitude of tolerance being taken advantage of; we as forgiving Christians must work through our feelings of self-righteousness, and give to the Holy Spirit what we cannot handle ourselves. We know God's rules and just like the brother, we feel the rug has pulled out from under us. Maybe this is a good thing; it forces us to realize the fine line between self-righteousness and God's righteousness. We find our base in God, through forgiveness and love; humbleness is the key.

("It was right that we should make merry and be glad, for your brother was dead and is alive again, and was lost and is found (NKJV Luke 15:32).

Holy Spirit Pray

> **Action** Help us to realize, God, we are all sinners, shaken and loved by You.
> Thank You, for humbleness of soul.

Wisdom

And the grace of our Lord was exceedingly abundant, with faith and love which are in Christ Jesus (NKJV 1 Timothy 1:14).

Grace hands us a way of staying away from religion of laws; with dos and don'ts. Religion does not give us, spiritual value; we cannot use it to earn our way into Christ's and God's Kingdom.

The only way to God's Kingdom is through grace; forgiveness of sin and purity of soul; obedience of God's will; which is purity of soul.

Believers use laws as a vessel to learn and know God, which structures our lives, accordingly. Satan can do this, also, and He probably does. Unlike humans, Satan cannot have purity of soul, through the Holy Spirit and grace.

God is a very wise and omnipotent God; He knows what He wants and He does it, His way; with true wisdom.

(Now to the King eternal, immortal, invisible, to God who alone is wise, be honor and glory forever and ever (NKJV 1 Tim 1:17).

Holy Spirit   Pray

Action   We should be thankful to God; He works out His plan for humanity;
And faithfully keeps His word. We have a beautiful God; A God
That keeps us safe from evil. Let us REJOICE.

Holy Spirit

And in the same way-by our faith-the Holy Spirit helps us with our daily problems and in our praying. For we don't even know what we should pray for, nor how to pray as we should; but the Holy Spirit prays for us, with such feeling that it cannot be expressed in words (Life Application Bible Romans 8:26).

Jesus sent the Holy Spirit to us (Acts 2:1), as a gift from Himself and God; He is God living within our soul.

The Spirit has many different characteristics: Truth, love, understanding, wisdom, mercy, and this is just the beginning. He is a teacher, a comforter, a counsellor, and much more; giving you guidance from Jesus for your life.

The late Dr. Kennedy, from Coral Ridge Ministries, has said, "The Holy Spirit is a person: He has a personality." * We learn this is true, as we deal with the Spirit in our lives daily. Once we know Him, we learn He is to be trusted; He is the Spirit of Truth.

(In the beginning God created the heavens and the earth... the Spirit of God was hovering over the face of the waters (NKJV Gen 1:1,2).

Holy Spirit   Pray

> **Action**   Thank God for such a unique gift as the Holy Spirit.
> God knows what we humans need.
> He knows how to help us live a better life.

*(Taken from the Coral Ridge Ministries, Dr. D. James Kennedy).

His Voice

"Most assuredly, I say to you, the hour is coming, and now is, when the dead will hear the voice of the Son of God; and those who hear will live" (NKJV John 5:25).

Jesus said His people would know His voice (John 10:4). Which means, when we have a personal relationship with Him, and the Holy Spirit, we listen for His Voice; it comes in many ways through truth. Reading His Word, doing His Word, and expressing His Word; helps to learn and know Jesus and who He is, so, when He speaks; we know.

Many times, He speaks through the Holy Spirit, who dwells among us. We are unified by the Spirit of God; which helps us to mature in knowledge, conscience, wisdom, understanding and the list goes on and on.

People build walls of pride, ego, ignorance, arrogance, lack of knowledge with possible evil intent. When we are ready to tear these walls down and face truth, God's Truth; we can listen for Jesus' voice.

("Are you a king then?" Jesus answered, "You say rightly that I am a king. For this cause I was born, and for this cause I have come into the world, that I should bear witness to the truth. Everyone who is of the truth hears My voice.")

(NKJV John 18:37)

Holy Spirit Pray

> **Action** Listen for Christ's voice by facing the truth; with love for our fellow-man.

Grace

For the law was given through Moses, but grace and truth came through Jesus Christ (NKJV John 1:17).

Moses revealed the laws on stone tablets, with rigid demands and strong justice.

Jesus reveals God's will and purpose to us, through blessings of forgiveness, love and understanding; unmerited favor.

He helps us realize, it is not our faith that brings God's blessing as much as it is His great faithfulness toward us and for us, that we are blessed; undeserved favor.

In other words, God loves us and once we ask for forgiveness, we are considered pure and He gives us Grace; willingly, thanks to our savior, Jesus and what He did.

Grace gives the power of the Holy Spirit to meet evil tendency within each of us. *

("And I will pour on the house of David....... the Spirit of grace and supplication; then they will look on Me whom they pierced (NKJV Zech 12:10).

Holy Spirit   Pray

> **Action**   Let us learn to love God as much as He loves us.
> Let us return His love and not let Him down.

*(Taken from the book, "If not for the Grace of God," by Joyce Meyer).

Time for Christ

The Lord helps them and saves them from the wicked because they run to Him.

(CEV Psalm 37:40)

How much time is spent with political ideas and thoughts? It is good to be involved with country and community, however, it is also necessary to remember God comes first; then our Christian friends, no matter what their political party. We must pull together in truth and in Christ.

Instinctively, we know good from evil. Building walls and becoming politically self-righteous creates idols.

What about our loving caring Christ? How much time do we give to Him? One hour a week; two at the most; ten percent of our day or 0% of our day? Would 5% of the day be fair? That is about one hour and fifteen minutes a day. Is it unfair to ask a busy person to spend that much time feeding their hungry soul? ASK GOD!

(The Lord protects His people and they can come to Him in times of trouble.)

(CEV Psalm 37:39)

Holy Spirit   Pray

Action   Let us allot a time for Christ; He deserves it;
So, do we.

Redemption and Forgiveness

In Him we have redemption through His blood, the forgiveness of sins, according to the riches of His grace (NKJV Eph 1:7).

Paul Harvey tells an Easter Story*

Reverend S.T. Gordon was walking when he saw a young boy holding a bird cage with little birds inside the cage. He asked the young boy, what are you going to do with the birds? The young boy responded; He was going to play with them for a while; then he would probably take them home and feed them to his cat.

Rev. Gordon asked how much he would take for the birds; maybe $2.00? Yes, I will take $2.00; then the boy took off down the street. Rev. Gordon took the cage; opened the door, letting the birds out.

Then Rev Gordon said, "Jesus and Satan were having a conversation. Satan said he had baited a trap; caught people in his cage; and now he (Satan) was going to have fun with them. He was going to tease them, play with them; Then he was going to deceitfully destroy them. Jesus asked "How much do you want for them?" Why would you want them, was Satan's reply? They will spit on you; put nails in your hands, beat you. I will take all your tears and blood!

Jesus said, "OK." He, Jesus took the cage and opened the door.

Holy Spirit   Pray

    Action   Christ went to the cross for us; what other God has done this for His people? He is a caring God!

*(As Heard on Bott Radio, April 5, 2021)

Approach

He who has the Son has life; He who does not have the Son of God does not have life. These things I have written to you who believe in the name of the Son of God, that you may know that you have eternal life, and that you may continue to believe in the name of the Son of God (NKJV 1 John 5:12,13).

We must be sensitive in our approach to Jesus Christ. He is joy; and in His presence He is complete peace. He is love beyond control. Faithfulness and humbleness are His favored attitudes; indescribable justice is His name. Beloved by all who abide in Him.

Jesus should be approached with humble respect: meaning a clean and purified soul of forgiveness, which takes away invisible wall building and lack of love. This creates an immeasurable life; eternally.

(Whoever believes that Jesus is the Christ is born of God…)

(NKJV 1 John 5:1)

Holy Spirit   Pray

Action   Know the name of Jesus; Repeat it often.
Respect Him; He is our God and King. He is our future. He loves us.

Citizenship

Now therefore, you are no longer strangers and foreigners, but fellow citizens with the saints and members of the household of God.

(NKJV Ephesians 2:19)

When we choose Jesus Christ and the Holy Spirit, we have chosen to become a citizen of God's family; chosen to habitat with God. There is no better place to dwell; no safer place to carry out duties, privileges, and rights.

God gave us a beautiful physical country to do exactly this; we need to stand up for Christ; to hold on to our country and our status of citizenship in God's family.

Let us stand up for Christ; if not, we lose both, God, and country.

(Stand, therefore, having girded your waist with truth, having put on the breastplate of righteousness... (NKJV Ephesians 6:14).

Holy Spirit Pray

   Action Stand up for Christ's truth and righteousness; Pray

Heaven

"Enter by the narrow gate; for wide is the gate and broad is the way that leads to destruction, and there are many who go in by it. Because narrow is the gate and difficult is the way which leads to life, and there are few who find it.

(NKJV Matthew 7:13,14)

We must fall in love with Jesus Christ; meaning putting Him on TOP of our Christmas tree, not ON the tree; No! The TOP of the tree! We have a lot on our tree; family, friends, work, etc. Jesus is first. If you are serious about God, and you want to go to heaven; be very sincere about following His word. Fall in love with Christ; it is not hard to do! Submission and obedience to His word is the key.

The Bible is truth. Scoffing it off saying it is old; is the rude thing to do. The Bible with its contents of character, integrity and moral law is an absolute; meaning there is no age limit. The Bible will live forever!

JESUS is the FUTURE.

(For the bread of God is He who comes down from heaven and gives life to the world (NKJV John 6:33).

Holy Spirit   Pray

   Action   The Bible is the Gospel; Let us follow it.

Vanity

The wicked in his proud countenance does not seek God; God is in none of his thoughts. His ways are always prospering; Your judgments are far above, out of his sight; His mouth is full of cursing and deceit and oppression; Under his tongue is trouble and iniquity (NKJV Psalm10:4,5,7).

Pride and vanity in wicked people are hard to deal with. It seems God allows them to prosper and get away with a lot.

We need to keep ourselves in the correct perspective, as to how we look at wickedness compared to God's humbleness. The wicked do not understand the punishment coming; we need to pray for them, with understanding and humbleness in love.

In praying, the evil just seems to disappear; including the vanity.

(You rescue the humble but you put down all who are proud.)
(CEV Psalm 18:27)

Holy Spirit Pray

Action Stay with God; Appreciate our beautiful God for what He does for us. Pray for the proud.

Natural Laws

Jesus said to Him, "I am the way, the truth, and the life" (NKJV John 14:6).

There are many natural laws in the Bible; the Constitution points this out as we learn about God and our country. This is one of the underlying themes of our Constitution and the Bible. The natural law of self-defense, the natural law of owning our home or property, the natural law of freedom and life, and it goes on.

We see this underlying theme in many of Jesus' statements; He is saying trust Him. He will break-down the invisible walls of fear to be able to see and feel truth. This in turn will bring us into the natural laws of life.

Our Founding Fathers trusted Him when developing our country, and look what a beautiful unique country we are perfecting. When we stay in the presence of Christ, we see our Constitution in a living, breathing way, with underlying natural laws of truths, which open the pathway to true life and freedom.

(For Christ has not entered the holy places made with hands, which are copies of the true, but into heaven itself…. (NKJV Hebrews 9 24).

Holy Spirit   Pray

> **Action**   This is true in our personal relationship with Christ and our personal pathway to heaven's life.

Jesus' Resurrection

"Behold, I lay in Zion a chief cornerstone, elect, precious, and he who believes on Him will by no means be put to shame" (NKJV 1 Peter 2:6).

Over half of our country have invisible walls built-up against any feeling for Christ and what He accomplished, by going to the cross for human salvation.

With these built-up invisible walls, these people follow any sophistry form of pretention. This seems to satisfy and fulfill a false sense of desire. A desire to be better than; or to be included in a sophisticated world of fallacy.

With this kind of coldness, it would be hard to feel the impact and compassion needed to appreciate the horrific, horrible pain Jesus suffered for mankind.

This callous attitude is; they have no need for Christ.

But God has His plan; We can see, He is in control, and Jesus was resurrected.

(You are followers of the Lord, and that Stone is precious to you. But it isn't precious to those who refuse to follow Him (CEV 1 Peter 2:7).

Holy Spirit Pray

> **Action** You are a group of royal priests and a holy nation.... Now you must tell all the wonderful things He has done (CEV 1 Peter 2:9).

The Son of God

But when He again brings the firstborn into the world, He says:

"Let all the angels of God worship Him."
(NKJV Hebrews 1:6)
But God says about His Son,
"You are God, and You will rule as King forever!"
"Your royal power brings about justice."
(CEV Hebrews 1: 8)

This is God's plan; His plan for our salvation. He predicted this and He kept His word (Ezekiel 36:24,25,26).

The Lord does everything the proper and orderly way. First, He gave us the Ten Commandments, which was a basic covenant between God and His people. This first covenant was the seed or root of the plan.

Then came the second covenant which was God's Son, Jesus, who said He was the Vine (John 15:5) and we are the branches.

The Ten Commandments gives us a righteousness in our relationship with Jesus: Jesus' royalty brings about justice.

(Everything written in it (the law) must happen (CEV Matthew 5:18).

Holy Spirit   Pray

   Action   The Ten Commandments are very important to learn, live and always keep them in our mind. Jesus is our savior; Let us live His Word (Jer 31:33).

NOTES AND REFLECTION

And they were all filled with the Holy Spirit and began to speak
with other tongues... as of fire, and one sat upon each of them.
(Acts 2:4,3)

....

....

....

....

....

....

....

....

....

....

....

....

....

....

....

....

....

....

Pentecost

When the Day of Pentecost had fully come…. and suddenly there came a sound from heaven, as of a rushing mighty wind… Then there appeared to them divided tongues as of fire………. And they were all filled with the Holy Spirit…

(NKJV Acts 2:1,2,3,4).

What is the believer's relationship with the Holy Spirit? A few years after Pentecost, the Holy Spirit swept through the whole world; filling all who had put their faith in Christ.

The Apostle John wrote, "By this we know that we abide in Him, and He in us because He has given us of His Spirit (1 John 4:13)."

With the Spirit, many times are special feelings; joy, true happiness; hunger for the word of Jesus; hunger for fellowship of Christ; the Spirit will let us know if we are doing wrong or thinking wrong. He, the Spirit builds our conscience by strong regret or painful sorrow. We should take the time to realize our feelings. The good thing about feelings; we pray and God answers.

(For by one Spirit, we were all baptized into one body.)

(NKJV 1 Corinthians 12:13)

Holy Spirit   Pray

   Action   Pray that we can identify with our feelings.

His Time

Grace, mercy, and peace will be with you from God the Father, and from the Lord Jesus Christ the Son of the Father, in truth and love (NKJV 2 John 3).

There is a saying, "The Christian life is not hard; it is impossible to maintain." God is a very wise God; with His wisdom He knows how hard it is for mankind to obey the rules. He knows how creative and adventuresome mankind can be; how boredom can lead off the path of righteousness toward God; to selfishness and self-centeredness.

God sent His Son to fix this problem; and He did. Jesus brought truth and grace. He went to the cross for this very reason; to save us from ourselves. With truth to help realize what we are doing; humbly we ask God for forgiveness. He will forgive us. The hard part is learning to forgive ourselves. It takes time and understanding, but truth and grace persevere.

This is part of our relationship with Jesus, who gives His Time for us to learn.

(I have no greater joy than to hear that my children walk in truth (NKJV 3 John 4).

Holy Spirit   Pray

> **Action**   It is our relationship with Jesus that makes our faith so wonderful and worthwhile.

His Gift

The wicked brag about their deepest desires. Those greedy people hate and curse You, Lord. The wicked are too proud to turn to You or even to think about You.

(CEV Psalm 10:3,4,).

I am sure we have all been around people with this kind of sad attitude. David pointed out in Psalms constantly, this behavior. It is good we see sinful behavior; because in the end, we have a beautiful God with great mercy; and we can, by His gift, grace, and the Holy Spirit, live in the presence of Jesus Christ.

(The Lord always does right and wants justice done. Everyone who does right will see His face (CEV Psalm 11:7).

Holy Spirit   Pray

    Action   Pray for all people, that they will accept His gift of Christ and the Holy Spirit. Pray they will see His face.

Acceptable

For you were once in darkness, but now you are light in the Lord. Walk as children of light, (for the fruit of the Spirit is in all goodness, righteousness, and truth), finding out what is acceptable to the Lord (NKJV Ephesians 5:8,9,10).

True Christianity comes when we learn what is acceptable to the Lord. Christ has given us the tools to find out what is acceptable to God. Test the (1 John 4:1) spirits. Ask yourself, are these people trying to persuade me to their cause; do they care about truth and being right in God's eyes; do they even know or care about the fruits of the Spirit? Do they care about integrity of the principles of God; or do they care about their cause?

We must be very careful as followers of Christ; are we listening to what is acceptable to Christ or are we listening to someone persuading us; moving in the darkness?

God is not a cause; He is a fulfillment. He is truth; His is our God.

(And have no fellowship with the unfruitful works of darkness, but rather expose them (NKJV Eph 5:11).

Holy Spirit   Pray

    Action   The fruits of the Spirit: Love, Joy, Peace, Longsuffering, Kindness, Goodness, Faithfulness, Gentleness, Self-Control (Gal 5:22).

Hypocrites

"Therefore, whatever you have spoken in the dark will be heard in the light, and what you have spoken in the ear in inner rooms will be proclaimed on the housetops (NKJV Luke 12:3).

We hear people say "I am a Christian," but yet they don't know what being born again means (John 3:3); how can they be a Christian without being born again?

We hear politicians say "I am a Christian," yet, when they give a speech at a Christian College, they cover-up the Ten Commandments (Mark 8:38); and vote God out of their conventions.

We hear voters say "I am a Christian," yet they vote for a political party, who has murder and power as their policy.

We hear colleagues say "I am a Christian,"; then they go home and listen ten hours a day, seven days a week, to a television station which has an antichrist influence (Matt 24:11) as their agenda. Oh, but they do go to church one hour a week; and the lists go on and on.

We wonder why we are losing our country to oligarchs, antichrists, and power-driven authoritative people.

Could it be that we are not putting our Christ first?

("Beware of the leaven of the Pharisees, which is hypocrisy" (NKJV Luke 12:1).

Holy Spirit   Pray

   Action   Jesus is the answer to it all; Stay in Christ's presence.

Heaven

Then as I looked, I saw a door standing open in heaven, and the same voice I had heard before, that sounded like a mighty trumpet blast, spoke to me and said, "Come up here and I will show you what must happen in the future!"

(Life Application Bible Revelation 4:1)

Just imagine a quiet, serene, still, smooth, translucent, clear, calm, transparent, PEACE; created by the Son of God.

Today, Jesus develops our character, our feelings and behavior; He deals with us as individuals, on a minute-by-minute basis, through the Holy Spirit (John 14:15). It will probably be the same relationship when He returns, taking His place as our leader and our God. Showing we love Him will be paramount; having faith in Christ will be easy. We will still have to follow and live truth filled lives; and trusting His leadership will be a must. There will be no evil, Christ has conquered the evil one; we will be protected totally from Satan's forces.

We can only imagine what life will be like, living with Christ; face-to-face. Kindness, consideration, love for God and our fellowman, abundant joy, goodness, humbleness, self-control, and the list goes on and on.

It will be heaven!

(… and I will give you the morning star (LAB Revelation 2:28).

Holy Spirit   Pray

Action   Stay with Christ; and receive the morning star.
Read Revelation 4:2-11.

Self-Respect

I have written to you, young men, because you are strong, and the word of God abides in you. And you have overcome the wicked one.
(NKJV 1 John 2:14)

Pride is something we can use for good or we can abuse and misuse it.

There are two types of pride; one is a pride despised by God which involves arrogance. So often this is the feeling that gets out of control by wicked people. People who reject and leave God out of their lives.

Then there is something called self-respect which we, as balanced human beings, enjoy because we are growing in our faith with Christ; who is at the helm of our lives.

Self-control plays a big part in our relationship with Jesus; so, does self-respect.

(....and the pride of life-is not of the Father but is of the world.)
(NKJV 1 John 2:16)

Holy Spirit Pray

   Action Abide in Christ, as we let Christ abide in us.

Kicking against the Goads

"Who are you, Lord?" Then the Lord said, "I am Jesus, whom you are persecuting. It is hard for you to kick against the goads (NKJV Acts 9:5).

Saul was a great leader for the monotheistic Jewish Community. A well born and bred Pharisee; a Roman citizen, who thought he was doing God's will, by killing and destroying the 'cult' called Christians.

On the road to Damascus to kill and destroy, Jesus stopped him dead in his tracks; He was blinded for three days. Christ woke him up!

Jesus works in wonderous ways; He is the Son of God who was worshiped as God, by Saul, who became Paul.

America seems to be kicking against the goads; simply because some of us cannot or will not face the truth of God. We are taken-in by 'Christian' oligarchs and 'Christan' antichrists with money.

We must pull together as Americans, and make our goal, God's truth! If not, will Jesus meet us on the road to Damascus?

(So, he, trembling and astonished, said, "Lord, what do you want me to do?")

(NKJV Acts 9:6)

Holy Spirit   Pray

> **Action**   Jesus is our God! He loves us. Pray, He will meet us on the road to Damascus. Pray that we will face the truth from God and pull together.

Self-righteousness

Also, He spoke this parable to some who trusted in themselves that they were righteous, and despised others... (NKJV Luke18:9).

Self-righteousness can be very dangerous as a Christian; followers of Christ. It is an attitude filled with pride, arrogance, and independence of Christ. It closes our minds to Christ's will. It develops our own will and our own selfish agenda in an invisible way.

After all of this, we develop an invisible wall between God's will and the way we want to do it. How do we, as followers of Christ, get back to God's will? The correct attitude.

We need to pray; to break down the walls of arrogance, pride and independence; to realize humbleness and how to soften our attitude toward others and to study our Bible every day.

We need to do everything we can to open our closed minds; to realize we need God!

(.... everyone who exalts himself will be humbled and he who humbles himself will be exalted (NKJV Luke 18:14).

Holy Spirit   Pray

Action   Let us keep our minds open to Christ by reading the Bible, praying, talking, and listening to the Holy Spirit; Face Truth.

Saint Peter

"You will know them by their fruits. Do men gather grapes from thornbushes or figs from thistles?" (NKJV Matthew 7:16)

In their arrogance, the elite on both sides of the aisle, have an attitude that they know better than God, what is best for our country. The person they want in the executive office, is for the elite's gratification, not the country's needs or the good of the people; or even God's will.

We wonder what really is going on behind the scenes or under the table. Is there such a thing as truth in our government? We know most bureaucrats have no accountability. We see people with money, have their hands in our elections and our government. This has been proven and covered up. We hear about some with selfish agendas, like Socialism, Marxism, Communism, Elitism, Caliphate, and the list goes on and on.

Nature always has a balance, most selfish agendas come back and hit where it hurts. The sad part is the innocent get hurt before the swing of the pendulum.

Our government has lost its conscience; it is called corruption. The people are not loved, cared for, or considered. We do not need an elite or selfish government.

We need Saint Peter back!

(Does not wisdom cry out!... "By me kings reign and rulers decree justice.")

Holy Spirit   Pray (NKJV Proverbs 8:1,15)

> **Action**   We need leaders that love the people of this country. Not the love of country for selfish purposes; like money and power.

Forgiveness

If you forgive others for the wrongs they do to you, your Father in heaven will forgive you. But if you don't forgive others, your Father will not forgive your sins.

(CEV Matthew 6:14, 15).

When we get hurt, we deal with feelings of repairing that hurt. The hurt brings on walls of resentment toward the people who hurt us. It brings about walls of anger and frustration toward ourselves.

Jesus wants us to talk this over with Him. He will help by letting us cast our cares over to Him. He expects us to realize, we are only human; the anger and frustration is very normal; this helps us to forgive ourselves, plus the people that hurt us. He does not want us to let these negative feelings turn into little idols of resentments, hurts, pain, anger, and frustration; which they often do.

Reconciliation is the next step; which is something you can talk over with God. This will be between you, God, and the one that hurt you. Reconciliation will be up to you and God.

We must forgive and let go!

(If we confess our sins, He is faithful and just to forgive us our sins and to cleanse us from all unrighteousness (NKJV 1 John 1:9).

Holy Spirit   Pray

> **Action**   This is the way we stay pure and holy in God's eyes. Let us realize this is the main way to stay in Jesus' presence. Then He will give you Grace. Grace be with you!

Friend

"If you abide in me and My words abide in you, you will ask what you desire, and it will be done for you" (NKJV John 15:7).

The boy had a dirty face; he had walked for miles just to be able to go to church. When he got there the door was closed; a man asked the little boy with a dirty face. what he wanted.

"I have walked a long while and want to come in." "No," was the reply, "you are too dirty."

The little dirty faced boy sat on the steps; very sad. He could not accomplish his mission. He could not go in because he was too dirty.

A car drove up; a big man got out and walked to the dirty faced little boy.

"What is the matter," He asked the little boy. "I can't go in because I am too dirty."

The big man held out his hand; the little dirty faced boy put his hand in the big man's hand; they together, walked hand in hand through the door, down the aisle, and the little dirty faced boy sat on the front row.

The big man, Rev. Moody went to the pulpit and began to preach. *

Holy Spirit Pray

   Action Stay in the presence of Jesus: He is our friend.

*As Heard on Bott Radio, by Anne Graham Lotz

The American Nation: The King of America is Jesus Christ

"Shall I not punish them for these things?" says the Lord. 'Shall I not avenge Myself for such a nation as this?' (NKJV Jeremiah 5:29)

If I were an antichrist, it would be a big feather in my hat to take over America. I would pay the media, who needs my money, to say bad things about Christianity; they don't have to be true just persuasive and convincing.

Since that did not work, maybe I would start paying people and set-up a bureaucratic government in America: Attorney Generals in special states; put key people in America's agencies, FBI, CIA, IRS, DOJ; take my pick. Then, convince or force certain companies to start an oligarch government; with me, at the dark hidden helm.

Since the Holy Spirit lives in the Christian body and the body is Christ's Temple, of course, I would have to take over Christ's Temple. I would have to force His people to worship me. Maybe by not letting them buy or sell food unless they worshipped me. Seems so easy! There is only one problem;

Christ has not spoken, YET....

(Who is he who over comes the world, but he who believes that Jesus is the Son of God?) (NKJV 1 John 5:5).

Holy Spirit Pray

    Action Pray for our Nation; Stay with Christ; He will take care of us.

Jesus Reads

"The Spirit of the Lord is upon Me, because He has anointed Me to preach the gospel to the poor; He has sent Me to heal the brokenhearted, to proclaim liberty to the captives and recovery of sight to the blind, to set at liberty those who are oppressed; to proclaim the acceptable year of the Lord (NKJV Luke 4:18,19).

We need at least two political parties in our country; if not we would end up with a dictatorship of Caliphate or Communist control. The people would no longer rule and get a free and fair election. This is very important. We have one of the longest running governments in the world, even though our country is young; because of our fair Constitution, thanks to the genius and Christian beliefs of our Founding Fathers.

Jesus has been our King in this country for over 400 years; the people realized their need for Him, and like He said He would, He answered their prayers abundantly.

We see what is happening today at our borders. People are coming in the mass to experience the abundance; simply because of what Jesus has given to this country.

The ignorant people who live here are destroying the very land they stand on. At this point in history, we have a choice; we can have our heads cut off; we can be locked in our homes and starve to death; or we can turn back to our God for His truth (2 Chron 7:14); He will gladly heal our land.

(Then He closed the book, and gave it back to the attendant and sat down (NKJV Luke 4:20).

Holy Spirit Pray

    Action Stay with Christ; pray with supplication for our country.

The Caliphate Wait

"I know your works, and where you dwell, where Satan's throne is. And you hold fast to My name, and did not deny My faith... (NKJV Revelation 2:13).

Shock and Awe! This was a way of showing American strength to the world. Within five years our economy had tanked, and we elected our first black Muslim president. Everyone was so proud of themselves; it showed we were not racist; the Caliphate Wait!

We took over Afghanistan for twenty years, and during that time our country has been divided to the point of total destruction! With Shock and Awe, we just won the battle not the war; the last twenty years have proven this; the Caliphate wait!

Iran has just about succeeded; and the Spiritual War of 'anything goes' has continued with the goal of winning their worldwide control of 'anything goes' for their god; the Caliphate Wait!

And do this, knowing the time, that now it is high time to awake out of sleep; for now, our salvation is nearer than when we first believed (NKJV Romans 13:11).

Holy Spirit Pray

    Action We certainly cannot call Americans racist. In our ignorance maybe, God will help us wake-up. Jesus Waits patiently!

Corruption

But these, like natural brute beasts made to be caught and destroyed, speak evil of the things they do not understand, and will utterly perish in their own corruption (NKJV 2 Peter 2:12).

We realize when we watch our government officials; they do not have the people's best interests in mind.

What they seem to be doing to enrich themselves, is taking money under the table: letting wars happen for profit; shutting pipe lines off for the benefit of other countries pockets and possibly their own; for personal insider trading; using other countries to advance their companies; making Americans suffer financial hardship for their profit; using their power to give to needy countries, so they can partition the sacrificial money from American citizens, and the tally goes on.

This seems to be happening in our government on all sides of the aisle. Watching television, putting two and two together, and reasoning out truth of this nightmare; knowing this could possibly be happening; are we going to have a good day? We will if we use our skills for His purpose, cast our cares to God, and stay in the presence of Jesus.

(They are spots and blemishes, carousing in their own deceptions while they feast with you (NKJV 2 Peter 2:13b)

Holy Spirit   Pray

> **Action**   Voting is extremely important, Stay engaged.
> Help God to help our country. Stay with Christ.

NOTES AND REFLECTION

"You are the world's seasoning, to make it tolerable. If you lose your flavor, what will happen to the world?"
(LAB Matthew 5:13)

....

....

....

....

....

....

....

....

....

....

....

....

....

....

....

....

....

....

SERMON ON THE MOUNT

Standard of Conduct

Great multitudes followed Him-from Galilee, and from Decapolis, Jerusalem, Judea, and beyond the Jordan (NKJV Mt 4:25).

Using the sermons on the hillside, Jesus has given us a standard of conduct to learn as His followers.

He shows us the difference between taking His path, which is how to relate to God and man, ethically and morally; compared to helping us understand the secular point of view.

He tells us how to conduct our attitudes in His faith of truth and love; compared to the way the Pharisees were interpreting the laws.

He, also, reminds us these attitudes and responsibilities for His followers have to be taken as a whole; we cannot just pick one or two and forget the others. Either you are His follower or you are not.

These attitudes are a basic vessel for us (Mt 5:19), to learn and grow in our faith of Jesus Christ.

("Let your light shine before men, that they may see your good works and glorify your Father in heaven" (NKJV Mt 5:16).

Holy Spirit   Pray

> **Action**   Jesus wanted His followers to always Glorify His Father; in attitude, in countenance, in conduct, in principle, in life. This is our first responsibility.

THE BEATITUDES

Blessed are the poor in spirit, for theirs is the kingdom of heaven. (v3)

Poor in spirit; Jesus is saying the poor in spirit have a need for God and they will receive it.

To Jesus happiness was not circumstances around us, on the outside; but it was joy and peace from within our soul; independent of what was happening in our situation of life; like pride and personal independence.

Jesus reminds us, if we pray to God with a poor spirit, God will change our attitude to a positive spirit of hope and love. To find hope is to get closer to the Lord and be willing to serve Him, obey Him, and to trust Him. Then our reward would be to receive the Kingdom from heaven into our soul.

God balances everything; those poor in spirit can be rich in faith.

("Follow Me, and I will make you fishers of men" (NKJV Mt 4:19).

Holy Spirit   Pray

Action   Even though the poor in spirit seem to be more serious with God's blessings; anyone can receive Jesus' rest in their soul. The key words are "Love Him."

THE BEATITUDES

*Blessed are those who mourn, for
they shall be comforted. (v4)*

Jesus is always with us (Mt28:20), even when we cry and grieve, we
do not ruin His day by our low moods or grieving spirit. He is, for
sure, our friend in need. We do not have to worry in talking to Him
about our inadequacies, our ineptitude, or our losing it with tears,
lots of tears.

He is always there to comfort us through the Holy Spirit; and take
care of us in our fears and our needs.

For a God, who is the Son of God, to be an omnipotent God of such
power and grace, He is there allowing us His time for us to weep;
and showing sustenance.

(Then when you realize your worthlessness before the Lord, He will
lift you up, encourage and help you (LAB James 4:10).

Holy Spirit   Pray

Action   We have a totally omniscient God. Let us stay in His
presence. Staying in His presence, helps us to teach
others; how to stay in His presence.

THE BEATITUDES

*Blessed are the meek, for they
shall inherit the earth. (v5)*

Jesus was trying to give these people hope in the presence of
despair. He was saying the humble shall have the land for their
own. Landlords were totally despised in Jesus' day. Hebrew scripture
teaches us that (Psalms 24:1) only God possesses the land. It is all
cultural. People that harvest the land year after year, knows only
God owns the land. Personal ownership is not necessary, but for
legal need or enjoyment. Most people understand, the land can
be taken from them by landlords or nature, at any time; Jesus tells
them that God is on the side of the humble. The message is: when
we get possessive of tangible things; so, often the thing we possess,
possesses us. *

(.. but the poor will take the land and enjoy a big harvest
(CEV Psalm 37:11).

Holy Spirit   Pray

   Action   God is always on our side when we practice fairness
              and justice.

*(Taken from the book, "Jesus' Plan for a New World, The Sermon
on the Mount, by Rishard Rohr and John Feister).

THE BEATITUDES

Blessed are those who hunger and thirst for righteousness, for they shall be filled. (v6)

We have two ways of looking at God's righteousness. One way is the attitude and actions God expects from us; the other way is to look through the eyes of God's truth and find the activity of God that brings about righteousness.

We hunger and thirst spiritually to be close to God. Lack of prayer and communication brings thirst to the surface. This helps us to realize our true desire is to be close to Christ's love, support, and unity with Him in the Spirit.

God's truth matters. For all Christians who have lived with the lack of truth realize how important truth is. Paul tells us (2Thess 2:10) to love truth; to believe only God's truth and it will save us from disdain; and it does!

Through God's activity of the Holy Spirit, we are filled with God's righteousness, His truth, and His love.

(Nothing is as wonderful as knowing Christ Jesus my Lord. I have given up everything else and count it all as garbage (CEV Phil 3:8).

Holy Spirit   Pray

> **Action**   For someone who came from hurting Christians to loving them through Christ, Paul is a good witness for Christ's love. Let us learn Paul's attitude.

THE BEATITUDES

Blessed are the merciful, for they shall obtain mercy. (v7)

Walls! Walls of indifference. Walls of dislike and malice. Walls of fear and pride to cover-up our inadequate feelings. Walls of arrogance.

Walls are everywhere, especially in our hearts. This is how the world deals with each other and themselves.

God's forgiveness works. He sent His beloved Son to deal with these intangible walls; and within three years, He did; through grace.

We need God; and with some of these invisible walls taken down, we start to understand. We start to have feelings again; and start having mercy for others.

Growing in Christ, we learn to have mercy for all.

(Blessed is he who considers the poor, the Lord will deliver him in time of trouble.

(NKJV Psalm 41:1)

Holy Spirit   Pray

    Action   We must stay in the presence of Jesus; it keeps the walls from forming. TRUST JESUS.

THE BEATITUDES

Blessed are the pure in heart,
for they shall see God. (v8)

When we keep a pure soul by getting close to God and ask for forgiveness as needed, it is very hard to understand deception of any kind. Lying, cheating, stealing, and covering-up the truth, and the list goes on; especially in our politics.

These people say they are Christians. They listen to lies, repeat the lies and believe the lies. Would we say these people are pure in heart? Would we say these people care if they are pure in heart? It is so hard to handle when we see this deception happening.

Our job is to love, care, and pray for these people and this situation; and to realize we will see God. God is in control!

(...)"so must the Son of man be lifted up, that whoever believes in Him should not perish but have eternal life" (NKJV John 3:14,15).

Holy Spirit   Pray

   Action   We cannot allow ourselves to accept deception and lies. Thank God for a beautiful Grace.

THE BEATITUDES

Blessed are the peacemakers, for they shall be called Sons of God. (v9)

When Jesus is talking about peacemakers, He is saying we should reconcile to God's word and to God, not necessarily to one side of an argument or the other.

It is written in the Bible that peacemaking is a must for a pure heart (Heb 12:14) and a clean life. In order to stay in the Grace of God, peace is imperative.

God's way of thinking, is the right way. We must keep Jesus and His teachings in the middle of the debate; or at least in thought; reconciling to Jesus as the referee. Therefore, we could be called the Sons of God.

Look at what is happening to our country; we must keep Jesus as our referee.

Keeping Jesus first is the key. If we allow some antichrist through television, to tell us how and what to think, we may end up in the middle of a Caliphate, with Sharia law as our referee.

In the history of America, we have kept Jesus as our King, and we have been peacemakers.

(It is never fun to be corrected. In fact, at the time it is always painful. But if we learn to obey by being corrected, we will do right and live at peace.)

(CEV Hebrews 12:11)

Holy Spirit Pray

Action Living in peace is God's way; the only way to freedom and growth, as a person, a nation, and a united universe under God.

THE BEATITUDES

Blessed are those who are persecuted for righteousness' sake, for theirs is the kingdom of heaven. (v10)

How STRONG is our faith? We are being tested!

In our WEAK commitments, we do not understand why being neutral cannot last forever. In our IGNORANCE, we cannot grasp, that we are made in God's image; which means we need God; or do we settle for any god.

In our ARROGANCE, we seem to believe we can do everything without God. Have we become our own little god? Remember we must have a god in our thirsting soul, this is how God made us.

In the year 2012, God warned us: "come to Me and I will heal (2 Chron 7:14) your land"; in 2016, He showed us how beautiful our land can be, by sending a serious righteous man, and the trash throwers tried to massacre the man. In 2020 the trash throwers got what they ask for; although the trash throwers do not realize it, yet. Ignorance!

Question: what happens to America now? Maybe God is leaving it up to the trash throwers. COME to Me, and I will heal.

(Yes, and all who desire to live godly in Christ Jesus will suffer persecution.)

(NKJV 2 Tim 3:12)

Holy Spirit Pray

   Action What does our thirsting soul tell us to do: throw trash or soften our hearts to Christ? Truth is what matters!

THE BEATITUDES

Blessed are you when they revile and persecute you and say all kinds of evil against you falsely for My sake. (v11)

God is Truth! This is what we have been saying through the whole book. Truth matters. Truth prevails. God's truth is what we want. God is the referee because real truth is what gives us the answer.

Some people do not want truth. They have their own selfish agenda and this agenda is their reality, but not God's truth. They must make fun of us; try to discredit us or what we stand for, since it is not what they want.

This is the danger, to listen to television propaganda; It is not truth; the propagandists cannot face truth. Find really real truth and you will find the God of this universe. God is Truth!

(Which of the prophets did your fathers not persecute? And they killed those who foretold the coming of the Just One, of whom you now have become betrayers and murders (NKJV Acts 7:52).

Holy Spirit Pray

Action God has prevailed when made-up religions have come and gone. He will be here forever, just like He has been here forever. These made-up religions will disappear. Turn off the television! Read Bible.

THE BEATITUDES

*Rejoice and be exceedingly glad,
for great is your reward in heaven,
for so they persecuted the prophets
who were before you. (v12)*

The Beatitudes are 2,000 years old, and yet they are still true today.

We have a right to rejoice and be glad, because time and age alone, show Jesus is the Son of God.

The problem is some people are in their own reality; some cannot face truth, or they make-up excuses of cold invisible walls, for not facing God.

The Bible, with all its proof of truth is the source of our faith. Jesus is everywhere in the Old Testament and the New Testament of true love. With all the back support of the Bible, a person could not possibly face truth, without seeing Jesus as the Son of God.

(These things I have written to you who believe in the name of the Son of God, that you may know that you have eternal life, and that you may continue to believe in the name of the Son of God (NKJV 1 John 5:13).

Holy Spirit   Pray

Action   We must pray; God will open their minds and show them the love of God; which is Jesus Christ, the Son of God.

Light on a Hill

"You are the salt of the earth; but if the salt losses its flavor, how shall it be seasoned? It is then good for nothing but to be thrown out and trampled underfoot by men (NKJV Mt 5:13).

Jesus reminds us, we are the salt of the world. He lets us know, we are the real leaders of the world; and asks us point blank: What happens when we lose the strength of our faith in God?

We must let the world see our light for Christ. Never let it blend in with the world; to do so, would make us totally worthless. We are of no value to our Father, if we do not make a point of letting the world know for that which we stand; Jesus Christ and God within His Glory.

("You are the light of the world. A city that is set on a hill cannot be hidden.)

(NKJV Mathew 5:14)

Holy Spirit   Pray

   Action   Stand BOLDLY for Christ!

The Perfect Son of God

"For many will come in My name, saying, 'I am the Christ,' and will deceive many"

(NKJV Matthew 24:5)

Jesus warned many times while He was on earth, cronyism would be practiced by other religions, which try to use His name for credibility. If it were true that Jesus is part of these loose religions, then He, Jesus, would be a hypocrite and He is not a hypocrite! Jesus is the Son of God, who treats us as individuals; and has kept His word. He would not be conspiring and consorting with any religions, or meeting with their leaders, who believe, through loyalty to their god, can and do lie, cheat, deceive, mislead, and so on; if it is for their god's purpose. Most of these religions believe in the five principles of evil. Christianity is against this evil.

Jesus, the Son of God does not practice cronyism with any religion. He requests that our souls be kept clean and pure through the truth of our omnipotent God.

It would be wrong as Christians to believe Jesus would commit any sin. Stay with the Bible; Christ is a serious, beautiful, perfect Son of God, whom God loves.

(And Jesus answered and said to them, "Take heed that no one deceives you.")

(NKJV Matthew 24:4)

Holy Spirit   Pray

> **Action**   Our love for Christ is sanctified; because He proves He loves us!

Out of Our Comfort Zone

"I will instruct you, and teach you in the way you should go; I will guide you with My eye" (NKJV Psalm 32:8).

The Holy Spirit is recognized by feelings; therefore, an understanding of the next step is getting the job done.

Starting down the wrong path creates silence in deafening tones. It is almost like someone is speaking, but not in a verbal sense. Praying with supplication, then waiting as patiently as possible with strong prayer on the lips; wanting to run away by keeping something else in our mind, yet the Holy Spirit has led us to God's will.

So, we pray for peace to replace apprehension, and we let go-giving all to Christ.

Understanding our feelings; we start the job again. Once again, we feel confident! Knowing we have drugged our feet to long; We ask, "Do we lack faith in our Christ? How do we do this job God, and where do we go from here?"

In gentle silence God says, "Follow Me."

(And suddenly there came a sound from heaven, as of a rushing mighty wind, and it filled the whole house where they were sitting (NKJV Acts 2:2).

Holy Spirit Pray

    Action Listen for God's word and direction.

Civil Unrest

But there were also false prophets among the people, even as there will be false teachers among you, who will secretly bring in destructive heresies, even denying the Lord who bought them, and bring on themselves swift destruction.

(NKJV 2 Peter 2:1)

In the 1800's the slaves in our Southern states were kept ignorant by the Southern white planters so, they would not rebel against such oppression.

The white people and the black people in the Northern states were the ones who gave their lives to free the slaves in the South.

The news media today with their sly and clever way of keeping a lot of us controlled, are creating the same atmosphere. Do not fall for the gossiping, scapegoating, lying, games of control. They know what they are doing! They don't understand the consequences of the outcome, but they want to control.

We can never let this happen in our beautiful and God-fearing country again. How do we fight this ignorance?

Ask Jesus to help us out of our ignorant bubble and open us up to truth and Christ's way.

(Many will follow their evil teaching.... And because of them Christ and His way will be scoffed at (LAB 2 Peter 2:2).

Holy Spirit Pray

> **Action** Ask ourselves, do we live in Christ's truth bubble? If not; Pray.

Super Hero

Righteousness exalts a nation, but sin is a reproach to any people.

(NKJV Proverbs 14:34)

A comic strip character was created in 1938, called Superman. * This was a time people needed hope. The war was raging in Europe with Hitler growing in power and taking over many countries.

It is amazing how much Superman's character is like Jesus. Superman came from another world; he was found and raised by adopted parents, who protected him from the world. His stand was justice, and his lever was the American way of right over wrong. His miracle was to fly and show up at the correct time. He took care of a city in need.

Jesus lived with parents who took care of Him, and protected Him from the world. His stand was God, which is truth and justice for all. His lever was the Word of God; good over evil, right over wrong, truth over lies, love over fear, respect over hate. His miracles are too many to mention; Instead of flying, He ascended.

He did not wear a blue suit with a red cape; but He does bear a cross with a purple robe. He takes care of the world's needs. His is our hope and foundation. He is the Son of God; He is our Super Hero!

(He who follows righteousness and mercy, finds life, righteousness, and honor.)

(NKJV Proverbs 21:21)

Holy Spirit   Pray

    Action   Jesus is our God; our hope. He is too omnipotent to express. Respectfully enjoy Him.

*(As heard on Blaze T.V./ Unashamed.)

Principles of Christ

Therefore, you must be subject, not only because of wrath but also for conscience' sake (NKJV Romans 13:5).

During the period of Roe vs Wade, was a time for us to persevere and pass the test of time, money, and dedication to our God.

If we gave in and joined the crowd of 'this is my body,' we are showing our God an agenda against His will; A selfish, 'I want my way'; convenient attitude.

If we stayed with our conscience of life, for an innocent baby, even though, it was a difficult path to follow, and very inconvenient, we were standing for the principles of Christ.

The fight has just begun; it has taken a different path but a more democratic one. Let us get involved with our state government; Let us push forward those principles of Christ.

(Let love be without hypocrisy. Abhor what is evil. Cling to what is good.)

(NKJV Romans 12:9)

Holy Spirit   Pray

Action   But if anyone loves God, this one is known by Him (1 Cor 8:3). We are all treated as individuals by Christ and the Holy Spirit. Stay in the presence of Christ and the Spirit; Love edifies.

NOTES AND REFLECTION

Great and marvelous are Your works, Lord God Almighty!
For all nations shall come and worship before You....
(Revelation 15:3,4)

....
....
....
....
....
....
....
....
....
....
....
....
....
....
....
....
....
....

A Constitutional Republic

"The light of a lamp shall not shine in you anymore, and the voice of bridegroom and bride shall not be heard in you anymore.... (NKJV Revelation 18:23).

We have had a beautiful country for 240 years.

To have fair elections and a government 'by the people' democracy, we must have a two-party system of voting. Without the two parties, we would have a dictatorship; one party would overpower the other.

Neo-Liberalism and Neo Rinoism indicate by their actions, they would like to rid themselves of Conservative righteous thinking. They talk about values and stress democracy. Values can be a man-made idea to fit any narrative; we can value most anything. Democracy can be controlled by good or bad corrupt people; on both sides of the aisle. Politicians saying it is a democracy, does not make it true.

A Constitutional Republic tells us what our values, our boundaries, our laws, and our principles should be. This is the fair way to think for all Americans; it gives power to no political party. It gives power to 'we the people of God.' The Constitution is a tool to retain that power. An honest free press is another necessary tool for a truthful stay in the principles of the Constitution.

(For your merchants were the great men of the earth...... (NKJV Rev18:23b)

Holy Spirit Pray

> **Action** God can make this work for us; just ask Him! Please stay with Christ.

Natural Laws of God

For since the creation of the world His invisible attributes are clearly seen, being understood by the things that are made, even His eternal power and Godhead, so that they are without excuse (NKJV Romans 1:20).

Schools were started in this country, to teach our children about the Bible. It was competition with Europe, not to be ignorant about the Bible. Then came godless people and stained humanity; it is called neutrality.

We have natural laws in our Constitution that give us the right to defend ourselves, which are seen in our Second Amendment of the Bill of Rights. * The natural law of nature's God, is found in Jesus' Moral Laws and the laws of the Ten Commandments.

The children in our schools should have a built-in conscience; once this is taught to them, they will feel this way of thinking. We cannot take away their quilt from their soul with neutral attitudes, without replacing this quilt with vigorous caring. Now we take their quilt and give them nothing. Nothing that is intoxicatingly positive in return; No prayers, no God, no Ten Commandments, no Bible, no show of love, only neutrality. We are leaving them defenseless.

We are failing our God and our children!

(For the wrath of God is revealed from heaven against all ungodliness and unrighteousness of men, who suppress the truth in unrighteousness... (NKJV Romans 1:18).

Holy Spirit   Pray

   Action   Thirty-four percent of the Constitution is taken from the Bible. * Let us stay with Christ in keeping with the Constitution.

*(Taken from Constitution Alive, Hosted by David Barton and Rick Green).

Moral Clarity

Therefore, putting away lying, "Let each one of you speak truth with his neighbor," for we are members of one another (NKJV Ephesians 4:25).

The walls are high for a lot of us. Looking for truth with our friends and sharing our feelings and thoughts does not always get us to pure truth.

After Jesus's calling, it is our responsibility to develop a relationship with Jesus and face the truth with His, and the Holy Spirit's help. Truth equals facts plus: understanding, discernment, knowledge of God, and Jesus Christ, with the Holy Spirit; the Spirit of Truth.

Facts are lacking, they are ridged, cold, not movable and secular; but mixed with the integrity of the living God, understanding and discernment from the Holy Spirit; we find truth. Because God is truth; Jesus with His great wisdom is the Prince of Truth.

Keep reading God's word (Jere 24:7), the Bible, and talking to Him; Look to Him and stay in His presence of holiness and purity. God put a natural law of truth in us; it is called common sense (Eze 36:27). He will help tear down the invisible walls of ignorance, and lead us to truth.

(...does not rejoice in iniquity, but rejoices in the truth (NKJV 1 Cor 13:6).

Holy Spirit   Pray

>   **Action**   In order to know God, we must face His truth; openly and honestly; through prayer.

Busybodies

For we hear there are some who walk among you in a disorderly manner, not working at all but are busybodies (NKJV 2 Thess 3:11).

They seem to be in our face; smiling. They are everywhere doing what is necessary to get attention.

The truth is, they are probably extremely anxious and depressed; conniving ways to feel like they are on top and to be in control. These silly teenage games seem to be a religion for them; by observing busybodies, this religion is more of an idol; they think works for them.

Jesus, God, and the Holy Spirit could be in their hearts; but they have built their imaginary walls and only they can tear them down to let Jesus into their souls.

(... an evildoer, or as busybodies in other people's matters (NKJV 1 Peter 4:15).

Holy Spirit   Pray

Action   Thank God for opening our eyes to a beautiful relationship with Christ. But as for you, brethren, do not grow weary in doing good. (NKJV 2 Thessalonians 3:13)

Evil Spitting on our Country

… he is proud, knowing nothing, but is obsessed with disputes and arguments over words, from which come envy, strife, reviling, evil suspicions…

(NKJV 1 Timothy 6:4)

Remembering as a young adult, we had a two-party system in our country that seem to work. All were for true liberty and democracy for all citizens; what was best for the people of the country. The parties had the same goals in mind; just a little different way of getting there.

In 2007, attitudes changed. People called each other liars. Then they started scapegoating our presidents, name calling of the other party, saying divisive things about skin color and authoritative agencies; like the police. Our agencies in our government, no longer cared about honor and justice; calling American citizens names like terrorists. There is no accountability; or honor of job. There are no character traits in most of our government bureaucratic agencies; a lot lie. There are some who will not say or they do not know what a woman is!

Where did all this evil come from? After 911 happened, evil started spitting on our country. What happened on 911? Who is secretly playing in the shadows?

(.. useless wranglings of men, of corrupt minds and destitute of the truth, who suppose that godliness is a means of gain. From such withdraw yourself.)

(NKJV 1 Timothy 6:5)

Holy Spirit   Pray

> **Action**   The best thing that we can do as Christians is, stay close to our God.

Separation of Church and State

… because although they knew God, they did not glorify Him as God, nor were thankful, but became futile in their thoughts and their foolish hearts were darkened (NKJV Romans 1:21).

Originally there was no such thing in our Constitution as separation of church and state; a total twist of the truth; a way in winning God out of our schools. With this kind of win, we are teaching our posterity, seclusion. Neutrality of soul, does not give our children a conscience. It gives an opening to choose evil over good.

A conscience of soul, means we give our children a choice and respect of boundaries to make that choice. Those boundaries should always be on the side of love and God. Evil should never be an option.

Adults cannot fight evil. How do we expect our children to fight evil without the tools needed to fight with? They need a good conscience to guide them to the correct decisions. This conscience would be the best gift we could possibly give to our children; never an attitude of neutral or a choice of evil.

(Professing to be wise, they became fools (NKJV Romans 1:22).

Holy Spirit   Pray

Action   God is so wonderful; we must ask. He will help us solve these problems. Condemning guns, cars, knives, hammers does not give us a solution; God will!

Compassion

"Has no one condemned you?"
She said," No one, Lord"
"Neither do I condemn you; go and sin no more" (NKJV John 8:11).

Jesus is not saying to omit Moral Law or the Ten Commandments. He demands that we as His followers, follow both the Ten Commandments and HIs Moral Law. He knows in order to help ourselves to become pure and holy, we must for our own good and growth in spiritual maturity, keep these commandments.

He is saying He has compassion on us even though we make wrong choices. He expects us to realize what we are doing and stop!

With grace he offers forgiveness for these wrong choices; and He remembers no more. Do not take advantage of His kindness; it is not the thing to do! He shows He is a beautiful God. He shows He is love.

(Do not grumble against one another brethren lest you be condemned.)
(NKJV James 5:9)

Holy Spirit   Pray

   Action   Know; Doing God's will is for our own protection.

His Friend

"Therefore, whoever confesses Me before men, him I will also confess before My Father who is in heaven (NKJV Matt 10:32).

The last few years Christianity seems to have gotten a bad name from people who are ignorant of Christ, or they are listening to untruths.

If a person has not experienced Jesus or read any part of the Bible, they could not possibly understand His value to society; maybe they should; and then judge.

It is a shame in this age of information that people play such a strong role in the lack of wisdom. This seems to be why our country is changing to total chaos. God has to be our friend, and our King in this country; there is no one else qualified for the task; if not, we are the losers!

("And he who does not take his cross and follow after Me is not worthy of Me.)

(NKJV Matt 10:38)

Holy Spirit   Pray

> **Action**   Pray to God that we do not become shallow, coarse, vulgar or imbecilic. Be a friend to Jesus, He is our friend.

Culture of Killing

"For what profit is it to a man of he gains the whole world, and losses his own soul? Or what will a man give in exchange for his soul? (NKJV Matthew 16:26)

Guns do not kill people, cars do not kill people, knives do not kill people, hammers do not kill people; People kill people!

Without a conscience and with an empty sick soul; we are creating a very vulnerable helpless evil sphere, within our culture and our posterity. What is needed to help create a righteous and clear conscience, for these defenseless people to fight evil, is to see life through an eternal perspective.

These people are looking through a lens with a desperate viewpoint; they cannot fight evil alone and win. These children want to be killed because they do not understand what is happening and they do not know how to fight this evil. We need to make them understand, they are not alone. They need hope and encouragement, like so many others who have found this confidence in a loving, caring, wise, truth filled, understanding God; like our leader Jesus Christ.

Jesus wept (John 11:35).

(Then the Jews said, "See how He loved him" (NKJV John 11:36).

Holy Spirit   Pray

    Action   Jesus loves us; He has proven this over and over; like the cross. He is with us through the Spirit, every minute of every day. We must make our children understand this.

A Gift of Grace

.... but these are written that you may believe that Jesus is the Christ, the Son of God and that believing, you may have life in His name.

(NKJV John 20:31)

Grace is a divine influence operating in man; with Jesus came grace and truth. As Christians, we start as sinful people and move into a life with the Holy Spirit as our guide; this is not simply something we earn, but it is a promise from God.

To become aware and obtain the Holy Spirit, we pray and ask Jesus for God's will.

He will give you the Holy Spirit and grace. Commitment, responsibility, trust, truth, dependability; These you will learn as you get to know Him and realize, we live in grace; a gift from God.

(.... lo, I am with you always...... (NKJV Matthew 28:20).

Holy Spirit Pray

    Action Jesus is not a forceful God. Once you make the decision to accept Him, don't let go. The Holy Spirit cannot protect you, if you do; for your own good, you must obey and pray.

Character of Jesus

…. Add to your faith virtue, to virtue knowledge, to knowledge self-control, to self-control perseverance, to perseverance godliness, to godliness, brotherly kindness, and to brotherly kindness love (NKJV 2 Peter 1:5,6,7).

Peter is telling us just what James tells us (James 2:17). Action and hard work must come, after gaining faith in our God. You will grow spiritually into the Christian you need to be, to show love to others. We are saved through love for Jesus; you have to know God, and do His will; through the Spirit.

Learning virtue, patience and self-control, helps in the process of developing character like Jesus. As Christians, we have to obey Jesus' Moral Law.

(Grace and peace be multiplied to you in the knowledge of God and Jesus our Lord (NKJV 2 Peter 1:2)

Holy Spirit Pray

Action Know God's will by studying the Bible, and praying for spiritual maturity; stay pure in soul; obey His word.

Humble Victory

"For whoever is ashamed of Me and My words in this adulterous and sinful generation, of him the Son of Man also will be ashamed when He comes in the glory of His Father with the holy angels" (NKJV Mark 8:38)

"Our church is not ready for the Holy Spirit; they don't understand it."

As we think through this ignorant statement from someone who is being very honest; how are we to relate to this attitude? This statement came from a woman who claims to be a Christian.

So often people lose perspective as to what Christianity means. Going to church every Sunday, working hard for the church or a cause for the church, doing good to others, tithing; these are all good things, we find in good traditional people. Evil can sometimes be traditional. The Apostle Paul tells us, our bodies are the temple of the Holy Spirit (1 Cor 6:19). In meeting God's purpose, we cannot be ashamed of Jesus or His Holy Spirit. In being humble, why would we want to feel shame?

(Jesus goes even further, "but whoever speaks against the Holy Spirit will not be forgiven him… (NKJV Matthew 12:32).

Holy Spirit   Pray

> **Action**   Please be careful. If you don't understand the Holy Spirit, ask your Bible based Minister or pray to God. The Holy Spirit will help you understand.

A New Generation

"But to what shall I liken this generation? "And saying: We played the flute for you, and you did not dance; We mourned to you, and you did not lament." (NKJV Matthew 11:16,17)

People are starting to understand and see the whole world needs God! After seeing criminal activity on television, and experiencing inflation, recession and the pandemic in our own lives, it hits us all where it hurts.

When we pray, so many of us expect God to wave a magic wand and have our way over night; if that does not happen and we don't get our way immediately the thoughts come rushing with force; "There is no God," "God does not answer prayers," "God cannot be trusted "; and the lack of faith goes on and on. God does not get tested by people; people get tested by God. What right do we have to judge our God with such selfish strength? If we had more faith, we probably would not be in this situation.

So, here we are; what do we do? We need to pray and stay in God's word. We need to get involved with our government and VOTE! Patience is a virtue. Evil will disappear! God is sending us a new generation; 72% of teenagers* believe in pro-life; good sign. It will probably take a while; God moves slowly; don't give up!

He sent His Son for the very purpose of making us realize—He loves us!

("But wisdom is justified by her children" (NKJV Matthew 11:19b).

Holy Spirit   Pray

   Action   Let us read our Bible; history will show how God works. God is not microwavable; unless He needs to be. Stay with Christ.

*(Taken from The Building of the America Heritage, David Barton and Rick Green).

Peace

Instead of bronze I will bring gold, instead of iron, I will bring silver, instead of wood, bronze, and instead of stone, iron. I will also make your officers peace and your magistrates righteousness (NKJV Isaiah 60:17).

To be called children of God and to keep peace going in the world you must love without hypocrisy; abhor evil; be kind, rejoice in hope, humble in spirit, stay in prayer, repent and help others to find peace.

Personal peace is pursued without concern for the world's chaos. In peacemaking between humans; one is a winner and one is a loser. With faith in God's peace, we end up with both sides as winners; we need to stay with God's peace.

(Blessed are the peace makers for they shall be called sons of God (NKJV Mt 5:9).

Holy Spirit   Pray

Action   Pursue peace in the world and stay firm for Christ.

The Agrarian Setting

"The kingdom of heaven is like a mustard seed, which a man took and sowed in his field, which indeed is the least of all the seeds; but when it is grown it is greater than the herbs and becomes a tree" (NKJV Matthew 13:31,32).

As we read and study the American Documents every July, we realize there is so much involved in agriculture with our God and His natural laws.

In an agrarian setting, our Founding Fathers would have realized these laws, and applied them to our everyday lives as Jesus has done in the Bible through parables and wise statements of truths.

God is described in many ways as a farmer or a lover of the land. * Jesus describes God as a 'Vinedresser' (John 15:1-8). He supplies rich food for His people, especially in heaven (Amos 9:13). God, Himself, while traveling with the Israelites in the desert, gave us many natural laws of life; including the natural laws of nature, called the laws of nature's God; the Ten Commandments (Exodus 20).

(In the sweat of your face, you shall eat bread, 'till you return to the ground. For out of it you were taken; For dust you are, and to dust you shall return.)

(NKJV Genesis 3:19)

Holy Spirit Pray

> **Action** God seems to love everything that comes from the land; including humanity. Stay with God; He is our God forever; His laws of nature prove this.

*(Taken from the," Illustrated Dictionary of the Bible," by Herbert Lockyer, Sr.)

The Shame of January 6th

For the mystery of lawlessness is already at work, only He who now restrains will do so until He is taken out of the way... And then the lawless one will be revealed.

(NKJV 2 Thessalonians 2:7,8)

This was a political game to get political gain. The right side of the aisle are the globalist-oriented, part of the political party of tradition, with their base slipping into the path of disaster.

The left side of the aisle is in total chaos, and destruction, hanging on by their fingernails; trying desperately to look like they are in charge; which in fact they are a growing monster of ignorance. They have lost their base! Saying they care, when we know they have left Americans in solitary confinement for well over a year and a half; breaking the rules of the natural laws of God in Amendments six and eight of the Bill of Rights.

Their arms of leverage are reaching out in total chaos with no way back to any base of caring. Most of these arms are hitting evil, and going into a downward spiral toward ashes of disintegration.

Meanwhile, the Conservatives and the moderate Liberals are sticking with God as their base, but doing nothing with the leverage of the Constitution; VOTE!

(... that they all may be condemned who did not believe the truth but had pleasure in unrighteousness (NKJV 2 Thessalonians 2:12).

Holy Spirit Pray

    Action The Founding Fathers said the Constitution would be, just another piece of paper, unless we put it into action. Pray for the men and women, and their families who have been mistreated in this issue; EXPECT!

Confused Programmers

…if God perhaps will grant them repentance…. and that they may come to their senses and escape the snare of the devil, having been taken captive by him to do his will (NKJV 2 Timothy 2: 25,26).

Their need to reprogram others is a basic insecurity and lack of trust. If reprogrammed, we would feel like the programmers, think like the programmers, act like the programmers, and be senseless like the programmers.

There would be no threat to their agenda; no challenge to their security. They would have their way—and what is that way? There would be enslavement to have chosen the path of selfishness; killing babies, picking on small children and confusing them, as to who and what they are; making scapegoats of young adults to the point of committing suicide or wanting to commit suicide; going along with puissant seekers and if it looks bad---lie!

The object is to give the Elite power. The programmers just do not understand why they have reprogrammed. Maybe the programmers should do a self-analysis and get in touch with Christ.

(But shun profane and idle babblings, for they will increase to more ungodliness.)

(NKJV 2 timothy 2:16)

Holy Spirit Pray

Action Thank God, He gave us Jesus Christ; and God as our Base!

NOTES AND REFLECTION

Put on the whole armor of God, that you may be
able to stand against the wiles of the devil
(Ephesians 6:11)

Armor of God

Therefore, take up the whole armor of God that you may be able to withstand in the evil day, and having done all, to STAND (NKJV Ephesians 6:13).

In order to stand against the darkness of evil, Paul is telling us to put-on the:

Breastplate of righteousness,
     Gird our waist with truth,
          Shod our feet with the preparation of the Gospel of Peace,

In order to quench the fiery darts from the dark evil one;
          We have to carry the Shield of Faith,
           The Helmet of salvation,

And the sword of the Spirit; The Word of God.
Pray with perseverance and supplication in the Spirit;
          With Boldness-STAND.

> "Awake, you who sleep.
>   Arise from the dead,
>   And Christ will give you light" (NKJV Eph 5:14).

Holy Spirit Pray

    Action Christ needs His followers to do their job. Do not just watch!

ARMOR OF GOD

Belt of Truth

We are not fighting against humans. We are fighting against forces and authorities and against rulers of darkness and powers in the spiritual world.

(CEV Ephesians 6:12)

God knows we cannot fight evil alone; but obtaining the knowledge of how to fight evil is a very good thing to learn.

Paul in the Bible, gives us an idea of how to wear the armor of God so, in the end of the battle against darkness, we will still be standing boldly.

He talks about the girding of the belt of truth; Truth holds everything together. It will hold our faith, our hope, our perseverance, our understanding and our knowledge of what it takes to fight evil.

Evil darkness of lies, cheating, twisted truths and vicious attacks of domination and control, is all too familiar.

Working with the Holy Spirit and learning that our strength comes from Him, understanding God's strength, we learn to appreciate God's truth; for we know it all comes from our Lord.

(When the battle is over, you will still be standing firm (CEV Eph 6:13).

Holy Spirit Pray

> **Action** We must be bold; we must stand; there is no one else!

ARMOR OF GOD

Breast-Plate of Approval

…...let God's justice protect you like armor (CEV Ephesians 6:14).

Satan in his sophisticated and evil dark mind, would know where to hit to take away our protection; our protection of course is God, who with His breast-plate of righteousness covers our heart; the main source of our trust and self-worth.

In His approval of us, He shows He loves us; and remember, He sent His Son to die for us. This gives God, the mighty power within us, to boldly STAND.

(…...let the mighty strength of the Lord make you strong (CEV Ephesians 6:10).

Holy Spirit   Pray

    Action   Remember to always trust God. He loves us; knowing this gives us self-worth.

ARMOR OF GOD

Shoes of Peace

Your desire to tell the good news about peace should be like shoes on your feet.

(CEV Ephesians 6:15)

Missionary work is what Jesus had in mind when He told us to go everywhere in the world (Acts 1:8), and talk about Him.

With any progress at all, the mission usually gets at least one interruption from the dark side.

Paul, the apostle, can tell us about His experiences; of all the floggings, beatings, ship wrecks, and the bad food from the many jail cells; he persevered and stood boldly. At the end of his life, he wrote to Timothy saying, "But the Lord stood beside me..." (2 Tim 4:17).

(The Lord will always keep me from being harmed by evil, and He will bring me safely into His heavenly Kingdom (CEV 2 Timothy 4:18).

Holy Spirit   Pray

Action   Do we know what it is like to be a missionary for Christ? How many interruptions have we had lately?

ARMOR OF GOD

Shield of Faith

Let your faith be like a shield, and you will be able to stop all the flaming arrows of the evil one (CEV Ephesians 6:16).

We must as faithful servants of Christ, be prepared to defend what we believe, and why we believe it.

We cannot give into silly insults, or feelings of rejection from our peers, and from the dark shadows of life. It is easy to give in, and it is also, soul searching to find the defense we need to fight on. Learn how to stop the flaming arrows; we will encounter from the Prince of Evil.

Just remember, if we were not being successful on our mission, we would not have any arrows shot our way by the evil one.

(Never stop praying, especially for others (CEV Ephesians 6:18).

Holy Spirit   Pray

    Action   Our job is to continue our mission, and shield our faith by knowledge of what we believe, and why we have our faith.

ARMOR OF GOD

Helmet of Salvation

Let God's saving power be like a helmet…. (CEV Ephesians 6:17).

The Helmet of Salvation protects our minds from the doubt and hopeless feelings, being hurled at us by Satan.

All we have to do is remember the cross. Satan himself is involved in this, because this is something he cannot win against. He has already lost thousands of times.

Jesus Christ defeated him, and he knows it.

Jesus gave us salvation with the cross. Nothing will ever change what He did for us; the question remains; what will we do with the cross of Jesus; when we have the support of the Helmet of Salvation?

(Always pray by the power of the Spirit (CEV Ephesians 6:18).

Holy Spirit   Pray

Action   With all the support of God, Jesus and the Holy Spirit; we can put on Our Helmet of Salvation, and continue our mission for Christ.

ARMOR OF GOD

Sword of the Spirit

And for a sword, use God's message that comes from the Spirit (CEV Eph 6:17).

The sword is the only armor of God that is a true weapon. The sword of the Spirit is the word of God. The word of God should be what we as Christians, use for offense to Satan's power and his strength.

This is our offense; we should put the word of God in our souls, our minds, and in our hearts. This is our protection to use the truth of Christ for our defense, from evil lies and hypocrisy; our defense for temptations, is our offense of knowing God's word; Christ's loving cross; and the sword of the Holy Spirit of truth.

Pray that I will be given the message to speak, and that I may fearlessly explain the mystery about the good news (CEV Ephesians 6:19).

Holy Spirit   Pray

Action   BE READY! Pray that we can when needed, take the offense against the Prince of Darkness and win. Let God be God.

Religion Outside the Soul

"These people draw near to Me with their mouth. And honor Me with their lips, but their heart is far from Me" (NKJV Matthew 15:8).

We see so many people with crosses hanging in their car, bumper stickers; people going to church weekly but listening to lies from others and television; Yet, they are not familiar with, or do not experience Jesus' Holy Spirit. What they are experiencing is a religion that has been taught, or has been accepted by what they see others doing or saying.

As truth filled Christians, we cannot stay on this self-righteous path of vanity and pride filled independence.

If we do not feel the Spirit of truth in our soul, which is a deep love for Christ and His way, we are experiencing a religion outside our soul.

We are not in the presence of our Christ!

('And in vain they worship Me, teaching as doctrines the commandments of men.)

(NKJV Matthew 15:9)

Holy Spirit   Pray

   Action   After committing you soul to Christ, constantly stay on your knees and humbly ask our Lord to help you receive the Holy Spirit. Once you start, do not ever let go for any reason!

Gaslighting

They have turned against the Lord and can't be trusted…. Don't tell us what God has shown you and don't preach the truth. Just say what we want to hear, even if it's false… We don't want to hear any more about the Holy God…

(CEV Isaiah 30:9.10,11)

There was a very popular movie made in the 1940's. The husband had a strong coveting desire for the young lady's jewels: which were unknown to her. Six months into the marriage, he convinced her totally, she was the one who had problems; in reality, he was insane with greed for her late aunt's jewels.

This is happening in our executive government. They are trying to convince the American people, we have no inflation problems, no border crisis, no energy crisis; and now what is so spooky they 'flip off' a nuclear war crisis. Through the corrupt news media, they can accomplish their gaslighting techniques. They are gaslighting to the point of destruction. These problems are their responsibility. We must keep the Ten Commandments. Do not bear (tolerate) lying. Gaslighting and the blame game does not work in these positions of power. Deniability, lying to oneself, and to the American people should never be in this setting.

(… the Lord still waits for you to come to him…! (LAB Isaiah 30:18).

Holy Spirit   Pray

    Action   Because you despise what I tell you and trust instead in frauds and lies and won't repent, therefore calamity will come upon you suddenly, as upon a bulging wall that bursts and falls; in one moment it comes crashing down. (LAB Isaiah 30:12,13)

Propaganda

And that they may come to their senses and escape the snare of the devil, having been taken captive by him to do his will (NKJV 2 Tim 2:26).

Propaganda, lying, cheating, stealing, creates total corruption.

How does this happen in a beautiful country, that the Trinity is our King? Narrative; whomever controls the narrative in any country, more sooner than later will control the people's thinking and doing, in that country; we see this all the time.

Most antichrists know this. The people will be taken in before they realize what is happening; or will admit to themselves they got taken. Usually, it is too late. Antichrists have a way of hiding in the open shadows. They have a charming way of lying, cheating, stealing and inducing corruption until the conversion works. Whom do we know that claim they are a Christian and yet, do unchristian things; like cover the Ten Commandments when giving a speech.

This is so plain, and yet, we do not see! Why not? Propaganda!

(...In humility correcting those who are in opposition, if God perhaps will grant them repentance, so that they may know the truth (NKJV 2 Timothy 2:25).

Holy Spirit   Pray

> **Action**   Have you been lied to; stay on your knees until you
> hear from Christ. Turn off the television.

Sealed

Now He, who establishes us with you in Christ and has anointed us, is God, who also has sealed us and given us the spirit in our hearts as a guarantee.

(NKJV 2 Corinthians 1:21,22)

We are owned by Jesus Christ. He puts his brand upon us. The mark of ownership is a two-fold guarantee. His mark of ownership and the Holy Spirit in our souls, shows we belong to Him; a first installment of our relationship with Christ.

What is great about this guarantee, is we know Christ fulfills all God's promises.

What a beautiful relationship: no anxieties, no worries, no condemnation, no shame, no guilt, no evil desires; just sealed with the love of Christ.

(...the solid foundation of God stands, having this seal: "The Lord knows those who are His.... (NKJV 2 Timothy 2:19).

Holy Spirit   Pray

Action   Thank God that we have been anointed by God; we are special.

Pass the Baton

Now I ask you to make a promise. Make it in the presence of God, who gives life to all, and in the presence of Jesus Christ......Promise to obey completely and fully all that you have been told until our Lord Jesus Christ returns (CEV 1 Tim 6:13,14).

Two-thousand years ago, Paul the apostle, passed the baton to Timothy. Many of the older generation remembers how we went through a period of loving, caring Christianity. Some Christians were critical, but most were faithful, caring people, who had a strong faith for Christ.

Even the Hollywood set showed Christianity; at least that was the popular attitude to show to the public.

Now forty years later, we have a new generation; Some are Christian followers; some are not. The pews are empty. Our children are being indoctrinated with man-made secular rules which must be stopped. Christ is there for us; He was 250 years ago when our founding fathers in America asked for His help; now we have the greatest nation in the world's history.

We need to pass the baton with our faith in Christ, which needs to be said to the next generation. Watch for the Baton!

(Fight a good fight for the faith and claim eternal life. God offered it to you when you clearly told about your faith (CEV 1 Timothy 6:12).

Holy Spirit Pray

  Action Each generation has the responsibility to pass the baton. If we love Christ, we will take this responsibility; seriously.

Convenience

.... How much more shall the blood of Christ who through the eternal Spirit offered Himself without spot to God, cleanse your conscience from dead works to serve the living God? (NKJV Hebrews 9:14)

As a culture develops values come from many different sources. If we don't keep God first in our value system, we can and do develop strange values.

Convenience in our lives, is one of those values. Whatever is convenient is the way we think, instead of thinking of God's will over our will of convenience, we find it easier to go with our moment of liberty; no wear and tear, no struggles or problems and the list goes on and on. We ignore all problems, therefore, giving us our value of comfort.

As an adult, we lose our conscience and pass this value of convenience onto our posterity. Without the boundaries of God's righteousness, our children settle for the cheap and shallow value of convenience. Many times, in the Spirit of naught, these values become law.

(Choosing rather to suffer affliction with the people of God than to enjoy the passing pleasures of sin (NKJV Hebrews 11;25).

Holy Spirit   Pray

> **Action**   Keep God first in our lives, we will wake-up fifty years from now and Thank God that we did. Stay with Christ.

Unforgivable Sin

Therefore, I say to you, every sin and blasphemy will be forgiven men, but the blasphemy against the Spirit will not be forgiven men (NKJV Matt 12:31).

Blasphemy against the Holy Spirit is a very arrogant sin. It takes a totally foolish person to commit such a sin; a disrespectful, thoughtless, human being to reject such a Spirit as the Holy Spirit. Ignorance plays a big part in this role.

The sin is not forgiven because this attitude and behavior prevents repentance. They are refusing God's forgiveness. God is a very loving and caring God; a forgiving God.

With an attitude as this, it would take a long time to come back to the correct, mature way of Christ. It would take a great deal of perseverance on the part of the sinful human being that dared God in such a manner; but it is possible that God would test them to see if they are serious about trusting and loving Him.

(Your words now reflect your faith, then; either you will be justified by them or you will be condemned (LAB Matthew 12:37).

Holy Spirit   Pray

Action   Stay humble and respectful to our Holy Spirit and our God.

Supreme Court Decision

Therefore, my beloved brethren, be steadfast, immovable, always abounding in the work of the Lord, knowing that your labor is not in vain in the Lord.

(NKJV 1 Corinthians 15:58)

As we shout with joy and thank Jesus Christ, we realize the inspiring Bible is correct; Evil melts away and disappears.

Forty-nine years is a life time for some of us, but for God it is but a drop. This makes us realize God is omnipotent. He takes His time and moves very slowly. Looking back, we can see how He worked this miracle; how many people He put in place, with the correct attitudes; the courage of our previous President, our Supreme Court Justices and many others who have been fighting for this decision.

Our God is a great God; Thank God He believes in life. Twenty years from now we will not think of the evil, we will see twenty-year-old people on television, thanking the Supreme Court for their courageous decision.

("And this is eternal life, that they may know You, the only true God, and Jesus Christ whom You have sent: (NKJV John 17:3).

Holy Spirit   Pray

Action   Now we don't have to feel guilty; we now have the right to vote the democratic way! No socialistic ideology.

The Word of God

For the word of God is living and powerful and sharper than any two-edged sword, piercing even to the division of soul and spirit, and of joints and marrow, and is a discerner of the thoughts and intents of the heart (NKJV Hebrews 4:12).

So many people scoff at God and His power. Many are looking at God through a man-made lens; even people who consider themselves Christians; with hanging crosses and bumper stickers.

The really real Followers see the word, as strength of faith in our God. Jesus said we can move mountains with the faith of a mustard seed (Matt 17:20). How far out on a limb are we willing to go for our Christ? How often do we go out on a limb?

The Spirit in our soul is our base of unity with God and man; we stay in this base continually by grace. We, then, reach out with our levers to show love, give tithes, develop faith, do service, listen for truth, and on and on. Special service for Christ comes, when the Spirit can trust us with righteousness and truth.

("Now the parable is this: The seed is the word of God. ... those who, having heard the word with a noble, and good heart, keep it and bear fruit with patience.)

(NKJV Luke 8:11,15)

Holy Spirit Pray

> **Action** We need to ask, "Are we a bumper sticker Christian; or is our faith based in God's word?" Stay with Christ.

Cardboard Christian

We are of God. He who knows God hears us; he who is not of God does not hear us. By this we know the spirit of truth and the spirit of error (NKJV 1 John 4:6).

The cross was in the window hanging from the rearview mirror in the car. This person gave the impression they were in love with Jesus and they were Followers of Christ. The cross is symbolic of what Jesus suffered and what He accomplished for God and humanity.

The lady driving the car came in, sat down, and began to speak. Two words out of her mouth and it was obvious the television news program watched, and she repeats what they say. We know these voters make scapegoats out of people just to boost television ratings; but the question asked, is why this cross dangling in the car window that represents our omnipotent Son of God, and yet repeats the lies she hears? What is she doing to the name of Jesus? This is definitely an inept attitude; possibly a strong sin against Christ.

Jesus survived the cross and will always win in the end; it is just so sad to see such ignorance and indifference to Jesus' request to do God's will, and follow the ninth commandment of the Ten Commandments.

(They are of the world. Therefore, they speak as of the world, and the world hears them (NKJV 1 John 4:5).

Holy Spirit   Pray

    Action   Let us not follow people who are not of God, and has no interest in staying with His will and requests. Stay with Christ.

NOTES AND REFLECTION

But you are a chosen generation, a royal priesthood, a holy nation,
His own special people, that you may proclaim the praises of
Him who called you out of darkness into His marvelous light….
(1 Peter 2:9)

....
....
....
....
....
....
....
....
....
....
....
....
....
....
....
....
....
....

Generation

Then God blessed them, and God said to them, "Be fruitful and multiply; fill the earth and subdue it; have dominion over the fish of the sea, over the birds of the air, and over every living thing that moves on the earth" (NKJV Gen 1:28).

God created man to take care of the animals and the earth. God is not a mean God; He likes people; the Bible shows this to us over and over again (Gen 3:21) so He made man for friendship; thus, starting our testing and procreation.

He made Adam out of dust and in His own image; in His own likeness. But He produced Eve out of the flesh and bone of Adam. Adam called her woman; even though they were naked, they were not ashamed.

(Therefore, a man shall leave his father and mother and be joined to his wife, and they shall become one flesh (NKJV Genesis 2:24).

Holy Spirit Pray

Action It took a while for God to create Eve for Adam as his helper; but it is worth it to wait on God's blessings. No matter what, stay in Christ's presence and grace.

Degeneration

So, when the woman saw that the tree was good for food, that it was pleasant to the eyes, and a tree desirable to make one wise, she took of its fruit and ate. She also gave to her husband with her, and he ate (NKJV Genesis 3:6).

Temptation is not always preventable, but James tells us (James 4:7) to flee from evil and temptation; because we cannot win against evil alone. Temptation usually leads to this choice, if we give into temptation.

Like Eve, many times in our innocence, we fail to stand up to temptation. But God has given us grace to help us back to the baseline of our faith.

A lot is learned, maybe more than we want to know. Sometimes, we go so far off base, it is hard to come back to God. Just remember, if we do find ourselves off the path, come back to God's grace as quickly as possible.

Adam and Eve did not have Jesus' grace, but we do, and we need to learn how to stay within that grace; we need to learn to stay with Christ!

(Then the serpent said to the woman, "You will not surely die" (NKJV Gen 3:4).

Holy Spirit   Pray

    Action   Jesus talked more about lying than anything else; and now we can see why. We can trust what God and Jesus say. Stay with Christ.

Abraham

For the promise that he would be the heir of the world was not to Abraham or to his seed through the law, but through the righteousness of faith.

(NKJV Romans 4:13)

Abraham and his family, who were descendants of Noah's son Shem, moved from Ur of the Chaldeans, to Canaan. Through much testing Abram stayed faithful and obedient to God.

God kept His promise to Abram that He would make him the Father of many descendants. They had a great relationship; Abram staying faithful and obedient to God; and God staying faithful and obedient to His word.

After God changed Abram's name to Abraham (Father of Nations), Abraham became the founder of the Jewish Nation. God promised to keep their agreement generation after generation, and He has kept His word.

Through many generations, Jesus came through the bloodline of the Jewish people. We have the Jewish Nation to thank for giving us Jesus, who is changing the world.

(...through whom also we have access by faith into this grace in which we stand, and rejoice in hope of the glory of God (NKJV Romans 5:2).

Holy Spirit   Pray

    Action   Even though Abraham failed many times, his faith in God is what was important to God. It is the same with Christians. Through Christ; Christians are a seed of Abraham.

Moses—Purity of Soul

Now it was so, when Moses came down from Mount Sinai (and the two tablets of the Testimony were in Moses' hand when he came down from the mountain), that Moses did not know that the skin of his face shone while he talked with Him….behold, the skin of his face shone, and they were afraid to come near him.

(NKJV Exodus 34:29,30)

In realizing as humans, how pure is our God; Our obligation and responsibility is to keep our soul and heart clean and pure before Christ. To learn to do this daily is to do God's will. By thinking of God instead of ourselves, we will mature in our spiritual life.

This is the first step; there are many more steps to knowing God and learning to love Him the way He wants us to show our love to Him.

The Ten Commandments will give an umbrella of what God expects from us. The first commandment, "Thou shalt have no other Gods before me," gives the starting point of God's will; purity of soul.

("So, be ready in the morning, and come up in the morning to Mount Sinai, and present yourself to Me there on the top of the mountain" (NKJV Exodus 34:2).

Holy Spirit   Pray

> **Action**   Stand before the Lord with respect and a pure heart.
> He is our God; He has definitely earned it.

Jesus

"This is the covenant that I will make with them after those days, says the Lord; I will put My laws into their hearts and in their minds, I will write them,"

(NKJV Hebrews 10 :16)

God said, I will give everyone a new heart and let their Spirit grow strong within them (Eze 36:26). He kept His word and Jesus came 700 years later, with truth and grace; the Holy Spirit.

With the Holy Spirit helping to learn truth and grace, we start realizing God's plan for regeneration. Insisting on obedience until we can learn to love Him and others as we should, then learning always with Jesus at the helm.

God's purpose is to unify and save us from ourselves; Therefore, Jesus with truth and grace in the Holy Spirit.

(…then He adds, "Their sins and their lawless deeds I will remember no more.")

(NKJV Hebrews 10:17)

Holy Spirit   Pray

Action   Without Jesus this world would be nothing; He is our present and our future. God's plan has worked and will continue to work; our job is to love with all our heart, soul and mind; never let go.

Regenerate the World

I have sworn by Myself; The word has gone out of My mouth in righteousness, and shall not return. That to Me every knee shall bow, every tongue shall take an oath (NKJV Isaiah 45:23).

Archimedes from Syracuse, Sicily (Italy), lived in 250 B.C. He was a successful mathematician, scientist, mechanical engineer, and inventor; who proved many theories. He said, "Give me a place to stand and I will move the earth."

Jesus in His wisdom and in His respect for God used God's word, and God the one who sent Him, to move the world.

This kind of foundation for us comes through the Holy Spirit. God is our place, as Christians, to STAND. With the help of the Spirit, we can move our boundaries out to meet our needs and others needs with the word of God. Jesus has given us a place to stand; the Holy Spirit within us and Himself. He has shown how to move goal posts, when necessary; with God's word; the Bible.

(That at the name of Jesus every knee should bow, of those in heaven, and of those on earth, and of those under the earth, and that every tongue should confess that Jesus Christ is Lord to the glory of God the Father (NKJV Phil 2:10,11).

Holy Spirit   Pray

> **Action**   Together with Jesus' guidance, we will regenerate the world.

Regeneration

God has sent me....to tell His secret plan to you Gentiles. He has kept this secret for centuries and generations past.... And this is the secret: that Christ in your hearts is your only hope of glory (LAB Colossians 1:25,26,27).

How do we regenerate the world? In time as purified Christians, we will be led and learn the answer.

God helps those who help themselves. It is our world; we are responsible for our world, even though God owns our world. Through wisdom and courage, we must be open minded to Christ's leading. Grace seasoned with salt will give us the initiative to boldly go for Christ. Love mixed with the wisdom of doves and with strong discernment will get us to where Christ wants us to be; Regenerating.

(Rooted and built up in Him and established in the faith, as you have been taught, abounding in it with thanksgiving (NKJV Colossians 2:7).

Holy Spirit   Pray

   Action   It is not what Jesus can do for us; it is what we can do for Jesus. As President John Kennedy said, this is true for our country also.

Born Again

Jesus replied, "What I am telling you so earnestly is this: Unless one is born of the water and the spirit, he cannot enter the kingdom of God. Men can only reproduce human life, but the Holy Spirit gives new life from heaven, so don't be surprised at My statement that you must be born again.

(The Life Application Bible John 3:5,6,7)

Let us take this statement literally because it comes directly from Jesus. We must fall in love with Jesus and trust Him. In order to enter His and His Father's Kingdom, there has to be a spiritual rebirth; a new and stronger spirit, which is a gift from God.

Making commitments to do the will of God is extremely important to God when going through this process of being born again. The Holy Spirit will test us until He is sure that this commitment is going to be kept, and we mean what we say. The thing we must do is persevere; show God, we mean it. This may take a short while or it may take a long time.

In either case, we will be dealing with the Holy Spirit and this in itself, is an awesome experience. This could be one of the most exciting things in your life; to be born again.

(And all who trust Him—God's Son—to save them have eternal life, those who don't believe and obey Him shall never see heaven, but the wrath of God remains upon them them (LAB John 3:36).

Holy Spirit   Pray

> **Action**   To love and trust Jesus is what we have to learn to do, obeying is not enough. Stay with the faith in Christ.

Baptism

When He had been baptized, Jesus came up immediately from the water, and behold the heavens were opened to Him, and He saw the Spirit of God descending like a dove and alighting upon Him (NKJV Matthew 3: 16).

Jesus was baptized! Why? He was the perfect man. He was and is the perfect God; so, why did Jesus want to be baptized? Most people are happy that Jesus was baptized. It shows support and leadership for His followers; especially now. He may have been showing us of His coming death and resurrection.

Jesus said to be born again with water and spirit (John 3:5). The water washes the body and in Jesus' case the dove which represented the Holy Spirit came to Him. A voice said, "This is My beloved Son, in whom I am (Matt 3:17) well pleased." This is one of those rare times that all three of the Trinity were together in one situation; the Father God, Jesus, the Son of God and the Holy Spirit, the third part of the Trinity.

Jesus evidently, thought it very important to be washed clean in soul and body, which we call sanctification and baptism.

(But Jesus answered and said to him, "Permit it to be so now, for thus it is fitting for us to fulfill all righteousness" (NKJV Matthew 3:15).

Holy Spirit   Pray

> **Action**   If you have not asked Jesus for forgiveness from your sin; then baptized, this should be a strong consideration.

Enslaved

Jesus answered them. "Most assuredly, I say to you, whoever commits sin is a slave of sin (NKJV John 8:34).

People say I don't want to be a slave to Christ with God's request that we trust and obey.

God created us just like He created the angels; free to choose. He created and spoke verbally, Himself the Ten Commandments; and put them on stone. The first commandment, "Have no other gods before Me" is saying, do not let idols of any kind enslave you and become your god.

God knows, we have to live with priorities; we must put Him first on our priority list. This strong structure teaches character traits, we need for growth of spirit. God is a living God; the Holy Spirit is alive and working within us.

Why would we want to be enslaved to a dead stone that doesn't talk or an intangible fad, which will be lost in six months.

The wise and mature thing to do is to have a beautiful relationship with a living God; Jesus Christ.

(He who is of God hears God's word... (NKJV John 8:47).

Holy Spirit   Pray

    Action   We have a gift from God; it is called choice! Let us use that choice and listen to hear Christ through the work of the Spirit.

Soul

Jesus said to him," You shall love the Lord Your God with all your heart, with all your soul and with all your mind" (NKJV Matthew 22:37).

Our soul is the principal part of our emotions. It is our deep feelings which needs spiritual nourishment, just like our physical bodies. We cannot deprive our physical bodies of food and water when we are hungry and thirsty, without suffering and burdening the body. We cannot deprive our soul of moral nourishment when we are spiritually hungry; without consequences.

Jesus Christ, who is the living word of God (John 1:14), God's Son, and the Bible which is the word of God, tells us our hunger and thirst of the soul can be satisfied by His eternal living water.

("but whoever drinks of the water that I shall give him will never thirst. But the water that I shall give him will become in him a fountain of water springing up into everlasting life" (NKJV John 4:14).

Holy Spirit   Pray

> **Action**   We have a God who fulfills our soul. Let's pray and thank Him, for caring enough to be our savior of our soul.

Humbleness

Let nothing be done through selfish ambition or conceit, but in lowliness of mind... (NKJV Philippians 2:3).

The Apostle Paul, in this verse, is writing about one of the Five Principles of Evil; a selfish agenda with an arrogant attitude.

As followers of Christ, we follow Him be reading His word and learning to have the same unselfish attitude as Christ. Being humble does not mean putting ourselves down; but instead, it means seeing ourselves in the correct perspective.

We are sinners, saved by God's grace and very worthy in God's eyes; and His Kingdom. We are a child of God---no one could be more worthy to be a child of God than someone who follows Christ. When we stay humble with Christ, He will take us out of our comfort zone and put us in a position that we love.

(Therefore, humble yourselves under the mighty hand of God, that He may exalt you in due time (NKJV 1 Peter 5:6).

Holy Spirit   Pray

   Action   Jesus says the first will be last, and the last will be first (Luke 13:30). Follow His lead no matter the circumstances; this is our moral responsibility. Lowliness of mind; Joy of heart! A leader!

A Friend

"However, when He, the Spirit of truth has come, He will guide you into all truth for He will not speak on His own authority, but whatever He hears He will speak; and He will tell you things to come" (NKJV John 16:13).

Jesus brought us truth and grace (John 1:17). When He started to leave us, He reminds us, that He will give us the Spirit of Truth which is the Holy Spirit.

As we read the scriptures and deal with the Holy Spirit on a daily basis, we realize, Jesus told us the truth about the Spirit: He never leaves us (John 14:16); He helps us in developing our conscience and shows us truth (John 14:17); He keeps us on the path of Jesus' righteousness (John 14:26) by pointing out our sins and our wrong thoughts. The Holy Spirit has been around (Gen 1:2) since the beginning of creation, but after Jesus left, He left the Spirit to abide within us (Acts 2) forever. With His many other attributes to our lives, the Holy Spirit is definitely the Spirit of Truth.

Jesus is probably the greatest friend anyone could ever have, since He left us with such a marvelous gift as the Holy Spirit.

("He will glorify Me, for He will take of what is Mine and declare it to you.")

(NKJV John 16:14)

Holy Spirit Pray

> **Action** Thank God for a friend like Jesus; such a friendship! We will never know another fulfillment like this again.

Globalism and Nationalism

For this is the will of God, that by doing good you may put to silence the ignorance of foolish men-- (NKJV 1 Peter 2:15).

We see the old Republican party as we watch on television the proceedings of January 6th sham trial. The leader on the right side, is a Globalist and as we see, she is trying desperately to destroy the previous president of the United States, because He is a Nationalist, who believes strongly in our Constitution and the people of our country. It is the American Constitutionalist that the elitists are trying to destroy. Most of us live for the Christian principles of our Founding Fathers; who believed in our country, our God and the Constitution.

The Globalist do not believe in our Constitution, even though they say they do. They seem to believe in a system of voting, which puts them on top; in power and control. They believe they should rule; they don't ask anyone else!

Our Nationalist God given Constitution is protecting us against Globalism; at least until 'we the people' wake up!

(…as free, yet not using liberty as a cloak for vice, but as bondservants of God.)

(NKJV 1 Peter 2:16)

Holy Spirit   Pray

    Action   Let us stay involved, with God first, in our government. Jesus will help us if we ask; Stay with Christ, so we can keep our country free.

Evil Salivation

"Fallen! Powerful Babylon has fallen and is now the home of the demons. It is the den of every filthy spirit and of all the uncleaned birds, and of every dirty and hated animal (CEV Revelation 18:2).

Not only do they try to reprogram to their way of thinking and away from You, God; but they are too ignorant to understand what they are doing. We can feel evil salivating as it works.

Israel is having the same problems as we are having in America, with evil working in their country and in their government. In March of 2017, a former president of the United States said he was going to Israel for their elections. Why would a former president go to Israel for the election? Now in 2022, they are having problems in their government. We can hear evil salivating as it works.

As we watch and discern fake trials against the people that love this country, the made-up and twisted lies are obvious. We can see evil salivating, as it works.

Unless You, God, step in and stop this evil salivation, renaissance humanity is dead; and we will return to more dark ages of human control and bubbles of ignorance.

(And the world leaders, who took part in her immoral acts, and enjoyed her favors will mourn for her as they see the smoke rising from her charred remains.)

(LAB Rev 18:9)

Holy Spirit Pray

> **Action** Our country is on the path of death unless we come to You in concerted measure, and stay with You, Jesus. We do not need human control; we need you, God.

Globalism

He shakes the earth out of its place, and its pillars tremble; Because our days on earth are a shadow (NKJV Job 9:6, 8:9).

According to the Bible, God has no plans for us to build a globalist Utopian government (Gen 11); a One-World-Order. He gives us countries, states, and power that will go to, 'We the people'; possibly for trial and testing of Jesus' way. We are only on the earth for an average of 80 years, which is but a drop for Christ. Christ, as our Leader and Ruler will want to know, what we are accountable for, in those 80 years.

This is God's planet, and Jesus is our future King and Ruler. We are only renters, as we squat on the earth. As humans, we are here to take care of our part of the planet, which would be impossible if our leaders are 10,000 miles away. They are only human, who are extremely susceptible to evil.

Jesus Christ is the only leader that has proven He can obtain this kind of leadership, so far away. He has achieved this and treats each of us individually, through the Holy Spirit.

(" For as the lightning comes from the east and flashes to the west, so also will the coming of the Son of Man be (NKJV Matthew 24:27).

Holy Spirit Pray

Action Stay with Christ; He is our leader through Spiritual and Civil Laws.

Appreciation

If anyone serves Me, let him follow Me; and where I am, there My servant will be also. If anyone serves Me, him My Father will Honor (NKJV John 12:26).

Jesus is our friend, our mentor, the love of our heart, our God; because of what He did for us. The Holy Spirit is our helper; our communicator; and our daily fulfillment of our soul. The Father God is our creator; He understands us better than we understand ourselves.

All three together make a Trinity of one God; helping man to grow spiritually in his heart; to discern strongly in his soul and to communicate with our omnipotent, omniscient, wonderful God; who evidently values us very much. With so much undeserved support given to us; we need to bow down every day and worship our true living God in appreciation.

(I have come as a light into the world, that whoever believes in Me should not abide in darkness (NKJV John 12:46).

Holy Spirit   Pray

   Action   Our God of the Trinity; we appreciate and honor You.

NOTES AND REFLECTION

But the Lord is faithful, who will establish
you and guard you from the evil one.
(2 Thessalonians 3:3)

The Beast of the Earth

Then I saw another beast coming up out of the earth, and he had two horns like a lamb and spoke like a dragon (NKJV Revelation 13:11).

We know if we put two and two together and reason out truth, we will understand what might be coming. We know our President is in the White House; many are asking who is in the Oval Office? Some say it may be our former president, since his people are working in the White House. Could it be our former president, and his buddy, the Atheist from Europe, are the two small horns, looking like a lamb, but acting and speaking like a dragon?

We know there was a debacle in Afghanistan. We were set up by our own government to look like the losers. Billions of American dollars were left behind, plus hundreds of our people got hurt, killed or left behind. The Caliphate wins!

We know a lot of evil men even in America, are sugar daddies for the antichrist. Maybe they are responsible for our open borders. The Caliphate wins!

We know America has sent $90,000,000,000 to the prolonged war in Ukraine; no one is allowed to ask how the money was distributed. Who wins!

We know Israel's Prime Minister was indicted and the government is being invaded by outsiders. It looks as though Armageddon is about to happen.

If so: We know Jesus is on His way here; or He is already here.

("Beware of false prophets, who come to you in sheep's clothing, but inwardly they are ravenous wolves" (NKJV Matt 7:15)

Holy Spirit   Pray

> **Action**   Let us cling to our guns and pray. Stay with Christ; He is our hope.

Dark Hole

"No one can serve two masters; for either he will hate the one and love the other, or else he will be loyal to the one and despise the other. You cannot serve God and mammon (NKJV Matthew 6:24).

We hear about evil antichrists buying a lot of Hispanic radio stations in Florida; they must have had the success that they desired, as we all can see with the television stations in our country. Now they want to hook these Christian Hispanics, coming across our borders with malice and deceit. If they control the narrative; they control our country with malicious evil.

The atheist seems to be a front man for his antichrist friends; their tail is as long as his, but they are hiding in their dark, dark hole. Who are his friends, or friend?

For the last 15 or 20 years, ever since 911, he and his friend or friends have been working in the shadows; which makes sense, since our country is so divided. We can feel and see the evil.

If they are allowed to stay in this country, we will lose our country. Some have already lost God, they just don't realize it, yet!

(Beware then of your own hearts, dear brothers, lest you find that they, too, are evil and unbelieving and are leading you away from the living God.) (LAB Hebrews 3:12)

Holy Spirit   Pray

    Action   Against such evil, stay with Christ. It is our only hope.

Flee

You are tempted in the same way that everyone else is tempted. But God can be trusted not to let you be tempted to much, and He will show you how to escape from your temptations (CEV 1 Corinthians 10:13).

If we don't flee and stay from temptation, there is danger of an evil trap. An evil trap which could end with lack of self-respect and lying to God. We cannot let ourselves, our minds, and our bodies be taken in by evil. Flee, by asking ourselves; are these people that I listen to Christians; or are they people taken in by atheists and antichrists, who are against Christ? We must stay away from desire and temptation and remember it no more; but we, also, must know where evil is coming from in our daily lives; and flee!

As the days go on, it gets easier; as our anger and frustration diminish. With God and with His help, we can, and do defeat evil; and will continue defeating evil as long as we don't blame God or ourselves, and put the blame where it truthfully should be, on the people creating the evil; and flee!

(Even if you think you can stand up to temptation, be careful not to fall.)

((CEV 1 Cor 10:12)

Holy Spirit   Pray

   Action   Stay pure by staying in the presence and grace of God.

Lucifer

Your heart was lifted up because of beauty; You corrupted your wisdom for the sake of your splendor; I cast you to the ground... Therefore, I brought fire from your midst; it devoured you (NKJV Ezekiel 28:17,18).

Angels have choices between good and evil just like humans do; God made us this way. God created the angels, just like He created humans.

Lucifer is not an equal or opposition to God; He was like all angels created by God. According to Dr. Jeremiah on Bott Radio, he was an angel of perfection; perfect beauty, perfect intelligence, perfect wisdom; perfect to the point of pride. He wanted to take God's place, God's position, God's power, God's glory and God's privilege. *

Lucifer was the head of the Cherubim angels, and when the fall came, one-third of the angels fell with him. Lucifer, by this time had become Satan and many other names; he wanted more. So, through the antichrists who walk and do business on the earth, Satan causes a lot of evil for all of us; especially in our government.

What is the answer? THE CROSS!

(Then you can say to future generations, "Our God is like this forever and will always guide us (CEV Psalm 48:13,14).

Holy Spirit   Pray

>   **Action**   Stay in the presence of Christ. Hold on with all of our heart, soul, and mind. Christ is the future!

*(Taken from Bott Radio, Dr. David Jeremiah).

Selfish Ambition

Don't be jealous or proud, but be humble and consider others more important than yourselves (CEV Philippians 2:3).

As a follower of Christ, we must be Christ-like in our thinking and our choices.

"I am entitled" or "I have a right because it is my...."

"We have our liberties and our freedoms to do what we want."

This sounds like the political parties in our country.

Yes, we do "have a right" and yes, we have "our freedoms" as long as it is under God's rule with His word.

Look for the truth of God, do not listen to other people and their beliefs. They will lead you down a path of regret. Listen to the Spirit of Jesus by reading and praying; Trust in Him.

(Pride goes before destruction and a haughty spirit before a fall.)
(NKJV Proverbs 16:18)

Holy Spirit   Pray

Action   It is our responsibility to find the correct path to Jesus. The Spirit will help find that path of truth in Christ. Everyone in our country should be based in this truth; without it we cannot understand each other and be unified.

Trust Jesus

Offer the sacrifices of righteousness and put your trust in the Lord.
(NKJV Psalm 4:5)

As we mature in our Christian faith amazing things happen in our lives. Growing by listening to God's Holy Spirit; one of these things is how we look at life and judge or understand other people. Usually, we see the world and others through our own eyes or through the world's eyes. This could be dangerous, if we see our truth through the world's eyes and believe it.

Maturity comes through letting go of our self-righteous comprehension, and start seeing people through God's eyes. Then we don't judge others so strongly. Leaving the judging attitude behind, and understanding what another person is saying, through listening to the truth of God, becomes very important.

We find real truth by praying and trusting Jesus.

(And we have such trust through Christ toward God
(NKJV 2 Corinthians 3:4).

Holy Spirit   Pray

> **Action**   Our attitude should be to trust and believe in Jesus completely.

God's Prophet

Love should be your guide. Be eager to have the gifts that come from the Holy Spirit, especially the gift of prophesy (CEV 1 Cor 14:1).

To be a prophet in any setting is probably a very hard thing to do. To be God's prophet is even a tougher job. Truth is the basis for any prediction. So, to see truth, a person would have to be close to God.

We need to study the Bible and pray, to be able to talk about Jesus and help others (1 Cor 14:4,5) to understand God's truth, so there are a lot of prophets in God's churches.

It is good to have spiritual gifts from God, especially if we as Christians, can help others to understand the message from Jesus; And to help stay with the Spirit of Christ through testimony of truth.

(They will realize that they are sinners, and they will want to change their ways because of what you are saying (CEV 1 Cor 14: 24).

Holy Spirit   Pray

> **Action**   Being clear with the message from God will help people to believe who God is.

Depart, Seek, Pursue

Come, you children, listen to me; I will teach you the fear of the Lord. Who is the man who desires life, and loves many days, that he may see good? Keep your tongue from evil, and your lips from speaking deceit. DEPART from evil and do good; SEEK peace and PURSUE it (NKJV Psalm 34:11,12,13,14).

The enemy of our soul, seems to show up in places not expected. It takes us by surprise; if not prepared. That is to say, we must build up defenses like: praying daily, reading the Bible, keeping our souls filled with God's word, and realizing who and how evil works.

Without God, fighting evil will be hard, if not impossible. With God at the helm, peace will come; Christ must come first, then our hungry souls will be filled.

(Let him turn away from evil and do good; Let him seek peace and pursue it.)

(NKJV 1 Peter 3:11)

Holy Spirit   Pray

Action   In order to satisfy the hungry soul, Jesus' truth must be pursued And we must seek the peace of God.

His Kingdom

Now after John was put in prison, Jesus came to Galilee, preaching the gospel of the kingdom of God (NKJV Mark 1:14).

Some people take offense to the word slave. God is not asking or telling us, we have to be His slave. Slaves carry the responsibility of their masters. They do everything physically, mentally, emotionally, and spiritually for their masters. They have to submit or punishment comes.

This is not what our God wants from us, or He would not have given humans and angels freedom of choice. From the Bible, He wants us WILLINGLY to keep our soul pure and holy; for His will is good over evil. Our will should be acceptance of God's way; for our own protection and growth of maturity.

"Have no other gods before Me," He wants first place in our lives; He created us. We need to have a god first; for our own good, He wants to be that God.

It is our responsibility to learn how to keep Him first. He shows us the way and gives instructions through the Holy Spirit, who gives us freedom to choose after much learning and reading the Bible.

Jesus tells us, and has shown us, how to receive His Kingdom.

(He said, "The time has come! God's Kingdom will soon be here. Turn back to God and believe the good news" (CEV Mark 1:15).

Holy Spirit Pray

> **Action** We need to accept Jesus and His Kingdom; it is a gift from God. God sent Jesus, and all He had to go through to give us this gift; Stay humble, don't turn it away!

Ask Christ

I tell you not to worry about your life… But more than anything else put God's work first and do what He wants. Then, the other things will be yours as well.

(CEV Matthew 6:25,33)

We all worry or at least, get concerned about things that happen. This is normal. Jesus is talking about hanging on to negative feelings which, by idolizing and hanging on to these negative thoughts, could turn into an idol.

Christ is a friend and a great God; He wants us to have a strong faith, realizing He will take care of us. We have to let go of our negativity of mind, and ask Him for positive thoughts, so we can grow and experience His abundance in our lives.

(Only people who don't know God are always worrying about such things.)

(CEV Mattew 6:32)

Holy Spirit Pray

Action We need to understand what a great God we have, and that He cares for us. Jesus is a wonderful, patriarchal God!

God's Guidance

O my son, be wise and stay in God's paths; don't carouse with drunkards and gluttons, for they are on their way to poverty. And remember that to much sleep clothes the man with rags (LAB Proverbs 23:19,20,21)

We as parents, need to wake up early in our children's lives, and learn how to pray every day for the direction of our children. Devotions daily with our family is so very important. Daily reading and understanding of what the Bible is saying helps them so much to make the correct choices in their lives; this gives them a base to grow from and keeps them strong.

The best gift we could give our children, is God.

(Don't envy godless men; don't even enjoy their company (LAB Proverbs 24:1).

Holy Spirit   Pray

   Action   Don't listen to grumbling from anyone; listen to God's guidance.

Purity

The refining pot is for silver and the furnace for gold, but the Lord tests the hearts

(NKJV Proverbs 17:3).

Purity is asking for forgiveness of sin; immediately.

When tough times come, we often feel like we are being tested. Testing helps clean out anything in our soul that is getting in the way of complete trust in God. With the realization that we are being tested, when situations start happening; or questioning these happenings, we can understand what Christ expects from us, and with positive prayer, we can learn to trust our God.

The testing makes us hungry for fulfillment of our soul; this in turn brings about an assertive attitude, which reading the Bible and praying helps to grow spiritually and more like Jesus. Trusting in God during testing makes Jesus very happy and it brings us praise.

(For He satisfies the longing soul, and fills the hungry soul with goodness)

(NKJV Psalms 107:9).

Holy Spirit Pray

   Action Stay with God during testing. In the end you will be refined and satisfied; Stay pure in Christ.

Gloom and Doom

"Then he goes and takes with him seven other spirits more wicked than himself, and they enter and dwell there; and the last state of that man is worse than the first. So shall it also be with this wicked generation (NKJV Matt 12:45).

We know evil can enter our bodies freely if we don't have the Spirit of Christ to protect us. This protection helps us to say no to the temptation (James 1:12) of evil. This is choosing God's will of freedom over sin of soul.

We have the wisdom to know arrogance and pride has no place in our soul; in order to receive God and His gifts of confidence and maturity. His Spirit of freedom, must be able to flow freely through our soul; therefore, clearing and cleaning for the positive love of God, rather than the evil, negative spirit of doom.

Through prayer and righteousness, we have found grace with our God today; so, therefore the Spirit of God can protect us from these spirits of gloom and doom.

Jesus was correct when He said, "You shall know the truth and the truth shall make you free" (John 8:32); free from gloom and doom.

("When an unclean spirit goes out of a man, he goes through dry places, seeking rest, and finds none. Then he says, 'I will return to my house from which I came.' And when he comes, he finds it empty, swept, and put in order (NKJV Mattew 12:43,44).

Holy Spirit   Pray

> **Action**   Let us keep our soul pure, clean, active and filled with Christ.

Demons

Now there was a man in their synagogue with an unclean spirit. And he cried out, saying, "Let us alone! What have we to do with You, Jesus of Nazareth? Did You come to destroy us? I know who You are--the Holy One of God.

(NKJV Mark 1:23,24)

Demons are actually evil spirits, probably in the same group as bad angels from heaven, that fell with Lucifer; Lucifer who is Satan. They seem to want more, in their tribe of evil.

The Bible does not describe how the evil spirit enters a person's body. It does describe how the person and the evil spirit in the body reacts to the purity of Jesus. They know, from what they say, who Jesus is. The fear through the voice shows the evil spirit within the man, is afraid of Jesus and His power. They should be afraid; He deals with them with the flip of His hand.

Satan did not create them, God created them. They have no power over God, but they do have influence in the human body; and they flip in and out of the human body very easily.

This is spooky; but it shows us how vulnerable we are as humans. The Holy Spirit protects our heart, soul and mind. We need God to fight and win over evil.

(For unclean spirits, crying with a loud voice came out of many who were possessed (NKJV Acts 8:7).

Holy Spirit   Pray

> **Action**   We as humans do not understand the spiritual world; but God does. Please stay with Christ!

Fire Breathing Dragon

Here is wisdom. Let him who has understanding calculate the number of the beast, for it is the number of a man. His number is 666 (NKJV Rev 13:18).

We hear on the news about an atheist, who hires Attorney Generals all over our country to represent our laws. The problem is, they seem to make their own laws; not the people's laws. This atheist seems to create a lot of problems in Israel, just like he is trying to destroy our country, America. He claims to be an atheist, who wants a One-World-Order. Is this why he is trying to destroy our country? Does this mean Caliphate or Communist rule? What really is meant by One-World-Order? Does this mean replacing Jesus as King of our world?

If this atheist is the dragon breathing fire, who is the human body called the antichrist?

(Who is a liar but he who denies that Jesus is the Christ? He is antichrist who denies the Father and the Son (NKJV 1 John 2:22).

Holy Spirit   Pray

Action   If this is the age of the antichrist, this is all the more reason to open our mind, heart and soul to Christ; by strong supplication and prayer. Jesus is the only one that can save us from this kind of spiritual evil.

Evil

But Jesus rebuked him, saying, "Be quiet, and come out of him!" And when the demon had thrown him in their midst, it came out of him and did not hurt him.

(NKJV Luke 4:35)

Jesus faced many demons while He was here on earth; with no fear, He treated them like they were a nuisance to Him and they probably were. Since we suspect they were fallen angels from heaven and ruled by Satan, they knew Jesus, and He more than likely created them. They feared for their future, with one snap of His finger, they would be gone. In the end that is probably what He did. The man himself was not hurt by the evil spirit, which shows their fear of Jesus.

What seems to be a nuisance for God is a real problem for us as human beings. We cannot fight this spiritual world alone. God knows this and has reached out to us through the sacrifice of our Lord Jesus Christ.

(Then they were all amazed…For with authority and power He commands the unclean spirits, and they come out" (NKJV Luke 4:36).

Holy Spirit Pray

> **Action** God is so good to us as humans; He does not treat us like we are a nuisance to Him at all. Jesus died for us on a cross; He did not snap His finger and destroy us; He loves us.

The Base of God

But put on the Lord Jesus Christ, and make no provision for the flesh to fulfill its lusts (NKJV Romans 13:14).

Even though Lucifer was the perfect angel, he still gets caught in his own trap. Lucifer is a perfect angel, who was thrown to earth without the Base of God. Every evil thing is OK to do as long as you do it for Lucifer; He has no base from God, only his own base of evil.

Jesus Christ, the Son of God, was put on this earth by God to give God and His Base to His people; which Jesus did, with the help of the cross, grace and truth.

He has sanctified us through the Holy Spirit in the Base of God.

The Base of God is all-natural Moral Law and the Ten Commandments; which is seen in our American Constitution.

(The night is far spent, the day is at hand. Therefore, let us cast off the works of darkness, and let us put on the armor of light (NKJV Romans 13:12).

Holy Spirit   Pray

    Action   Let us stay in the Light of Jesus, He is the Son of God; He is our God.

NOTES AND REFLECTION

"Amen! Blessing and glory and wisdom, Thanksgiving and Honor
and power and might, Be to our God forever and ever. Amen."
(Revelation 7:12)

Appreciation

"You will see the Spirit come down and stay on someone. Then you will know that He is the one who will baptize with the Holy Spirit" (CEV John 1:33).

Thanksgiving is a time to reflect on our lives, with things, people, and places that touch our hearts, with gratitude, inspiration and joy. We acknowledge that as God's people we are blessed to the point of abundance. What a gracious, caring God we have.

We owe a great amount of honor to just Jesus alone, not only for what He did for us, but for what He continues to give to us every day.

Other things and people are on our mind at this time of the year, but our core value of our faith and lives deserve a great amount of appreciation.

(I saw this happen and I tell you that He is the Son of God (CEV John 1:34).

Holy Spirit   Pray

    Action   Thank God for all that we have; Thank God for the Son of God.

A Giver

Meditate on these things; give yourself entirely to them, that your progress may be evident to all (NKJV 1 Tim 4:15).

Jesus was definitely a giver. There are movies that have been made that say there are givers and there are takers. Of course, these movies are secular, and they don't deal with our Christian faith, but if we had to define Jesus under their secular terms, He, Jesus would be described as a giver. He took nothing, and gave everything.

He showed us humbleness; from His birth to the humble way that he allowed them to present Him on the cross. Even when He was resurrected from death, He did not come back boastfully and say, "I told you so." No, instead He did His job and finished what He had started, humbly.

He is the Messiah, He is the Christ, His is the Son of God, and yet He gives.

He is definitely a gracious giver.

(...be an example to the believer in word, in conduct, in love, in spirit, in faith, in purity (NKJV 1 Tim 4:12).

Holy Spirit Pray

    Action We must follow our leader, Jesus the Messiah, the Christ, the Son of God.

The Good Samaritan

Then Jesus asked, "Which of these three people was a real neighbor to the man who was beaten up by robbers?" The teacher answered, "The one who showed pity" (CEV Luke 10:36).

We all know the parable of the Good Samaritan. The man traveling was beaten and robbed by thieves; the priest's attitude was to avoid the situation, the Levite looked curiously at the wounded man, and then passed on. It was the Samaritan, hated by the Jewish people, that offered compassion for the wounded Jewish man.

Ironically, Jesus Himself, ended up at the end of His life here on earth, showing pity and compassion for us. We were wounded from our sin and in total despair.

He showed, He was definitely a Good Samaritan.

(...Jesus said, "Go and do the same" (CEV Luke 10:37).

Holy Spirit Pray

    Action Jesus is our great leader, a God of action and compassion. The Living God within us.

Ministers Shout for Christ

… having your conduct honorable among the Gentiles, that when they speak against you as evildoers, they may, by your good works which they observe, glorify God in the day of visitation (NKJV 1 Peter 2 :12).

Americans today do not live in the same environment as Christians lived in the 1730's. We have television and the internet, to control us ten hours a day, with secular comfort and easy convenience; other religions consider us spoiled and say so. We are all sinners. We are not perfect; but we have lost our train; it seems to be backward. We desire evil (scapegoating, accepting lies, gossip), and we get it.

God is trying to wake us up! We have a beautiful God. He has given us so much. But we are controlled by secular television and the internet, not our ministers. How do we turn our train around, and get back to our God with His beautiful boundaries of the Ten Commandments and natural Moral Laws. We could start with prayerful realization of truth; committed engagement in helping our God, country, family and friends; in that order; strong sacrifice of wants and desires; painfully serious about goals toward a close personal relationship to God.

Would we show God, we love Him; instead of ourselves and our everyday idols of convenience? Maybe then our ministers would feel more comfortable standing for Christ Boldly.

(… though He was a Son, yet He learned obedience by the things which He suffered (NKJV Hebrews 5:8).

Holy Spirit Pray

> **Action** We can start the train rolling; the next generation could keep it at full steam. Christians and Ministers, let us stand boldly for Christ; and against this tyranny of division. Let us suffer for our Christ; He did for us. Turn from evil!

Snap

Then they took up stones to throw at Him; But Jesus hid Himself and went out of the temple going through the midst of them, and so passed by (NKJV John 8:59).

We know from reading the Bible that Jesus hung on a cross for us. Why did He do this? The answer is because He wanted us to know, He loves us and God loves us! Jesus did everything that God wanted him to do (John 6:38). Everything he did was to glorify God; How do we know this? Because He said so. Even now it is for us to see God' glorification.

In the Gospel of John, John tells us, when they were throwing rocks at Jesus; He hid. Where did He hide? Was it just a snap? And He was gone!

He went through the process to be hung on a cross to show us how much he thought of us. In this process His body was beaten nearly to death; they pounded spikes into His hands and His feet; He hung on the cross, naked, three feet from the ground, for hours, with people walking by Him saying things to shame Him; spitting on Him, His body died! Now, how much does He love us?

He was God, to end all of this, all He had to do was ---Snap!

(Therefore, they sought again to seize Him, but He escaped out of their hand.)

(NKJV John 10:39)

Holy Spirit   Pray

    Action   Our God and Savior loves us to an extreme; How much do we love Him?

Second Mission

He who rejects Me and does not receive My words has that which judges him---the word I have spoken will judge him in the last day (NKJV John 12:48).

Jesus' second mission to this earth will be to find out how we handled His first mission. After studying the Bible, how do we live on this earth with things like: sharing the gospel with others; how we treat others; how do we feel about others; how do we feel and treat Jesus, God and the Holy Spirit? How do we feel about ourselves and treat ourselves?

These are all things we should be learning from the Bible and from others; as well as our relationship with Jesus through His Spirit; the Holy Spirit.

On His second mission, He will be judging us. We will be receiving eternal life, if we lived and accepted His will (1Thess 4:15-18); compared to living however we pleased, which will lead to eternal punishment (Revelation 20:11-15).

This is something we should individually, strongly think about. After all He has been through for us; I think He is very serious.

(...for they loved the praise of men more than the praise of God.)
(NKJV John 12:43).

Holy Spirit   Pray

>   **Action**   Love God with all your heart, soul, and mind. Be strong; never quit.

Royalty

Therefore, since we are receiving a kingdom which cannot be shaken, let us have grace, by which we may serve God acceptably with reverence and godly fear.

(NKJV Hebrews 12:28)

Emanuel means "God with us." We are all individualists; we get treated by our Lord as individuals, who are listened to and our requests are addressed by the Holy Spirit; possibly by God's angels in heaven. With our soul full of the Holy Spirit and unified with Christ and other believers, this is God's church and His Glory.

Does this make us feel like royalty; it should, because we are dealing with royalty. Knowing this about the Lord; we should feel very humbled and grateful. Knowing our God cares so much for us, that He would treat us with such royalty and grace.

All we have to do is keep ourselves sanctified, by staying pure in spirit, in order to reach up to this level of God's royalty; Humbly

(...for so an entrance will be supplied to you abundantly into the everlasting kingdom of our Lord and Savior Jesus Christ (NKJV 2 Peter 1:11).

Holy Spirit Pray

    Action Stay with Christ's unified individualism.
               Stay with Christ's royalty and grace; Stay with Christ.

God's Purpose

For God so loved the world that He gave His only begotten Son, that whoever believes in Him should not perish but have everlasting life (NKJV John 3:16).

God wanted us to accept Jesus the Christ, His Son as our savior. That was God's plan and purpose, to save mankind from their sin. Jesus, while He was on earth, told us this over and over, to help us understand the relationship between God the Father and God the Son; and to understand the path to heaven. "I am the way, the truth and the life (John 14:6).

With purity of soul, trusting in God's word through the Bible and the Holy Spirit, and obeying Jesus' teachings; we are staying with God's purpose for our lives.

(.... No one comes to the Father except through me (NKJV John 14:6).

Holy Spirit Pray

    Action God keeps His word. It will always be that way. Trust our beautiful Omnipotent God and our precious Savior, Jesus. With this trust we will live a peaceful and good life.

The Holy Spirit

"So God, who knows the heart, acknowledged them by giving them the Holy Spirit just as He did to us" (NKJV Acts 15:8).

It is always amazing how the Holy Spirit works in us, through us, around us and for us. The Spirit answers our prayers right before our eyes; it is called awestruck. In my humble opinion, the Holy Spirit is the most powerful force on this earth.

In order to obtain the knowledge of how the Holy Spirit works, show Christ that your faith is strong and He will make known to you the Holy Spirit. Don't give up; He has to know you are serious.

To know we have such a precious gift as the Holy Spirit, is in itself, a miracle. A miracle from God to humanity. Who would not want such a miraculous gift?

("and made no distinction between us and them, purifying their hearts by faith.")

(NKJV Acts 15:9)

Holy Spirit   Pray

> **Action**   With Christ's boldness, pray that the Holy Spirit will assist us to witness for Christ. There are so many people in need.

Abide in the Light

Then Jesus cried out and said, "He who believes in Me, believes not in Me but in Him who sent Me." "And if anyone hears My words and does not believe I do not judge him; for I did not come to judge the world, but to save the world."

(NKJV John 12:44,47)

Jesus' message is clear; He came to draw us to Him. He came so people may see the light of God; showing them salvation, and the way to obtain eternal life.

He did not come to judge, condemn, or criticize, but to let us experience the Holy Spirit, who in turn shows us how to love and to have joy and peace. The Spirit helps us to learn to develop patience, kindness, humbleness, and the character traits of Jesus. He, also, keeps our hearts and souls pure like Jesus, so, we can abide in the light.

(I have come as a light into the world, that whoever believes in Me should not abide in the darkness (NKJV John 12:46).

Holy Spirit   Pray

Action   Let us study our Bible, so we may know and understand the character traits of Jesus; this is so important to Jesus. It shows Him, that we love Him and we are fair by giving back.

Pursue Peace

Let him turn away from evil and do good; Let him seek peace and pursue it. For the eyes of the Lord are on the righteous, and His ears are open to their prayers; But the face of the Lord is against those who do evil (NKJV 1Peter 3:11,12).

Peace sounds so good and so quiet; Peace is such a quiet place. It relaxes us to the point of total harmony in our soul. Our contentment comes with complete focus on amity; friendship with Jesus.

Love of our Lord gives us tranquility, security, the feeling of knowing we are, and will be taken care of in everything we do; or live.

Without our Lord, we are nothing to speak of; with Him, we have everything including peace.

(Finally, all of you be of one mind, having compassion for one another, love as brothers, be tenderhearted, be courteous (NKJV 1 Peter 3:8).

Holy Spirit Pray

>   **Action** Love, Joy and Peace is what comes from God, through the Holy Spirit. Thank God for all of His gifts.

Faith in God

Therefore, do not be unwise, but understand what the will of the Lord is: giving thanks always for all things to God the Father in the name of our Lord Jesus Christ.
(NKJV Ephesians 5:17,20)

Much praise should be given to our Lord; for He has done so much for us. He has given us so much we realize most of what He gives us is totally undeserved. He still gives generously; He keeps His word.

We should learn humbleness and graciousness before our gracious God. Jesus, who was sent by God, is our King. He is our rock and hope for the future; He is and will be our savior. Let us thank God for Jesus the Messiah.

The Holy Spirit is our everyday protector and helper of our faith. He helps us relate to our God, to others and to ourselves. Thank God for our faith in Jesus.

(Continue earnestly in prayer being vigilant in it with thanksgiving (NKJV Col 4:2).

Holy Spirit   Pray

> **Action**   Thank God for God; Thank God for Jesus our Christ; Thank God for The Holy Spirit. There is so much to be thankful for.

Sharing

What we mean is that God was in Christ, offering peace and forgiveness to the people of this world. And He has given us the work of sharing His message about peace (CEV 2 Cor 5:19).

God brings us back to forgiveness of sin and throwing away our sin, making us pure and holy through what Christ did on the cross. Having grace, gives us the righteousness and goodness of soul to reconcile to helping others, see God.

Having the trust for God and the Trinity (John 10:30), helps to share with others our feelings of love for God and Jesus through the Holy Spirit.

Sharing is an obligation to our faith, and the commandment Jesus made (Acts 1:8) just before He ascended to heaven. This is the way to meet God's Glory, in learning to share Jesus' teachings and His love.

(Therefore, do not be unwise, but understand what the will of the Lord is; submitting to one another in the fear of God

(NKJV Ephesians 5:17,21).

Holy Spirit   Pray

Action   Share with others God's message of love, so, God and man can be reconciled in love through the Holy Spirit of God.

Nature's God

"The Lord watches over everyone who obeys him, and He listens to their prayers. But He opposes everyone who does evil" CEV 1 Peter 3:12).

We have natural laws of nature's God, which is found in the Ten Commandments. Even though, we as humans just like animals would like to murder, commit adultery, steal, lie and listen to lies, and definitely covet; God says NO! He knows this would lead to total chaos and destruction of humanity.

This destruction is happening in our country today. We are totally into chaotic lies, listening to lies and scapegoating others. We are not pulling together in God's truth! It's as though, we are worshipping our political parties, rather than putting God and Jesus first. First in truth, forgiveness of others, love and the lists go on. Our country is more divided than it has ever been. Our leaders of are giving divisive speeches, our prejudiced media uses us to keep themselves afloat in their business, with no sign of remorse for their lies and scapegoating techniques; our government agencies and our people's house is totally off the wall with no accountability for their actions.

What happen to our Ten Commandments and our Constitution? According to them causing this chaos; they are seeking democracy; Gaslighting!

(For it would have been better for them not to have known the way of righteousness, than having known it, to turn from the holy commandment delivered to them (NKJV 2 Peter 2:21).

Holy Spirit   Pray

    Action   Are they bearing false witness? Stay with Christ! It is the only thing that makes sense during this chaos.

Participation

He who did not spare His own Son, but delivered Him up for us all, how shall He not with Him also freely give us all things (NKJV Romans 8:32).

Let us give thanks to our omniscient God, who is with us and within us, as we grow in our lives, and become aware of the need in our country for our participation and our action as our civil duty.

We realize as we forge ahead, and review the Constitution of our country that God has been with us from the very beginning; He helped form this beautiful sovereign state. We understand, as we study the Constitution, almost 50% of it was taken from the Bible and/or the writings of the men of faith in Christ.

From their writings, we know that our Founding Fathers knew Jesus and the

Holy Spirit, intimately. They share this relationship through their writings and participation in the Declaration of Independence, the Constitution, and the Bill of Rights.

Let us give thanks for such beautiful Documents from our Lord.

(Continue earnestly in prayer, being vigilant in it with thanksgiving (NKJV Col 4:2).

Holy Spirit   Pray

Action   Since there is so much twisted truth about the founding of our country, and the original intent, we need to study these papers. We need to know as Christians, the natural rights God gave us.

Glory to God

Now to Him who is able to keep you from stumbling, and to present you faultless before the presence of His glory with exceeding joy (NKJV Jude 24).

To comprehend our relationship with Christ during the season of Thanksgiving, we take a step back and examine our feelings and thoughts, in a reality of truth. According to Constitution Alive, truth is real, obvious, and does not change. *

As we reason out the truth of our relationship with God, we have to give thanks for His many blessings. Not only does He give us grace daily, but He through His mercy, gave us Jesus and the Holy Spirit; for the support that is needed in our daily walk.

With the Constitution of America*, God has blessed us with freedoms incomparable to any country in our world's history. As we share Thanksgiving with our family and friends, let us all reflect on the truth of God's Glory.

(To God our Savior who alone is wise, be glory and majesty, dominion and power, both now and forever… (NKJV Jude 25).

Holy Spirit   Pray

>   **Action**   Thank God for the Constitution. Like all things that
>   God has a hand in writing, it is the best.

*(Taken from The Constitution Alive, David Barton and Rick Green).

The Spirit of Goodness

Therefore, consider the goodness and severity of God; on those who fell, severity; but toward you, goodness, if you continue in His goodness. Otherwise, you also will be cut off (NKJV Romans 11:22).

Thanksgiving is a season of quiet reflection; making plans and setting goals; letting God know how grateful we are for all He has done, and is doing for our individual relationship with Him. Our intimate relationship that we cherish everyday of learning about God; experiencing the Lord in an awesome way of kindness and love; knowing Jesus is taking care of us is a great feeling of comfort and peace in the soul.

Thanksgiving is a time to share God with family, relatives, and friends. With God's help it is a time to see the goodness in a chaotic world of honorable, dutiful, and just men.

(… but glory, honor, and peace to everyone who works what is good…. For there is no partiality with God (NKJV Romans 2:10,11).

Holy Spirit   Pray

   Action   And let us consider one another in order to stir up love and good works (Heb 10:24). God is good all the time!

NOTES AND REFLECTION

For unto us a Child is born... the government will be upon
His shoulder.... His name will be called Mighty God....
(Isaiah 9:6)

Wholesomeness

"Do not think that I came to bring peace on earth. I did not come to bring peace but a sword (NKJV Matthew 10:34).

In this season of His birth, we become aware that Jesus did a lot of things to shake-up and wake-up humanity; that sword is the word of God. He expects us to use that sword. He knows what is needed in a world of ignorance and chaos. What He gave then, and what He gives now is individual attention to each; to clean and purify our souls. While He was on the earth, He helped the lame and the ill individually and with the help of the Holy Spirit, Jesus continues His work as He always has done.

The thing that sets Jesus apart is the individual attention (John 14:6), He gives freely to everyone who will follow Him and His commandments of righteousness and wholesomeness.

It is beneficial to us in this amorous season of love, to recognize what a great God and Spirit we have as leaders of men.

("Peace, I leave with you, My peace I give to you" (NKJV John 14:27).

Holy Spirit   Pray

   Action   Keep our God first, this is His commandment. Stay with Christ.

Heavenly Circle

And though I bestow all my goods to feed the poor, and though I give my body to be burned, but have not love, it profits me nothing (NJV 1 Corinthians 13:3).

Even though, Jesus is seen and felt in our lives of busyness throughout the year, we sometimes forget the feeling of such warmth and kindness, that is experienced during His birthday season.

Jesus is the lamb of love, which has left our world with a rebirth of new light that will shine forever. Every year the Spirit of Giving shines on everyone with such a strong realization of wanting to give; It seems to touch the Heavenly Circle of Love throughout the world.

(And now abide faith, hope, love, these three; but the greatest of these is love.)

(NKJV 1 Corinthians 13:13)

Holy Spirit Pray

Action But when that which is perfect has come, then that which is in part will be done away (1Cor 13:10). Let us stay with Jesus, the one who loves us.

Thoroughbreds

For Jews request a sign, and Greeks seek after wisdom; but we preach Christ crucified…. to the Greeks foolishness, but to those who are called, both Jews and Greeks, Christ the power of God…. (NKJV 1 Corinthians 1:22,23,24).

The Greeks were well trained in the things that mattered; they were thoroughbreds. They believed that teaching their posterity paideia, they would avoid outsiders or cruel dictators from coming into their country and dominating or enslaving them. They made this their base which protected them from this kind of invasion. They reasoned, if they had a deep knowledge of the things that mattered, no one could enslave them.

As God fearing people of righteousness our base is the Constitution, written through the Spirit of God which protects against invasion.

We see and hear on the news, how the antichrists and oligarchs are chipping away at the base of the Constitution. One of the chips is to turn our country against God; which has been happening to our children for 100 years.

Antichrists chip at our God given beliefs, our country, our laws, and through the media they malign us against each other. They use nasty names, scapegoating the opposite political party, the police, different skin colors, and the list goes on.

In order to save our country, we need to become well trained in the things that matter; we need to become thoroughbreds for Christ's way.

(… to the knowledge of the mystery of God…. are hidden all the treasures of wisdom and knowledge (NKJV Col 2:2,3).

Holy Spirit   Pray

    Action   Let us become thoroughbreds for Christ.

Harmony of Abundance

But we are bound to give thanks to God always for you, brethren beloved by the Lord, because God from the beginning chose you for salvation through sanctification by the Spirit and belief in the truth (NKJV 2 Thessalonians 2:13).

When we think of Christmas, we think of the Spirit of Christ; how warm and gracious Jesus can make us feel. The wonderful look of Christmas; the smell of pine cones, and the taste of eggnog by the fire; knowing we have a secure and loving Father, who loves us very much; who shows us the harmony of abundance.

We are so blessed in America, with God on our side. Let us realize this season, how to give to others, the way God has given to us; while we worship our Lord with giving and humbleness.

(Meditate on these things; give yourself entirely to them, that your progress may be evident to all (NKJV 1 Timothy 4:15).

Holy Spirit   Pray

Action   Give to our fellowman; Give to our God, always!

False christs

"For false christs and false prophets will rise and show great signs and wonders to deceive, if possible, even the elect (NKJV Matthew 24:24).

About 500 years after the birth of Christ, it became popular to plagiarize different religions and collect them into one religion. Many of these collective religions claimed Jesus was involved in their religion; which was totally untrue, unethical and an intentional deceiving lie.

Jesus would never be involved in evil. Putting Jesus' name in their made-up religion was done to make that religion sound authentic.

Some of their laws are evil based, which fit under the Five Principles of Evil; pleasure, to much pleasure; selfishness, thinking of self only; selfish agenda, a cause or idol for a selfish purpose, or a selfish god; greed, covetousness; and force, usually harsh and cruel treatment. Some of these older religions teach anything can be done for their god, as long as it is for his purpose.

Most of these religions had no natural laws of God; like the really real omnipotent God's Principles and Moral Laws. Jesus, the Son of the omniscient God, warned of false christs and false prophets many times. He falls into God's absolute.

("Then if anyone says to you, 'Look, here is the Christ!' or There!' do not believe it. (NKJV Matthew 24:23)

Holy Spirit   Pray

Action   We can reason out the truth of Christ from history; plus, the Bible and the works of the Holy Spirit.

God's Purpose

And we know that all things work together for good to those who love God, to those who are called according to His purpose (NKJV Romans 8:28).

The Revolutionary War had just started and in what is now, Trenton, New Jersey. The Hessians, from Germany, were celebrating Jesus' birthday by drinking wine and enjoying the day and night of Christmas. George Washington and his men were not celebrating Jesus' Birthday, even though they observed it. Yet, God seem to be closer to General Washington's thinking and on the side of America. George Washington won the battle with no loss of life.

They say Washington prayed five hours a day, and he probably was praying every step of the march on Trenton, that cold and lonely morning.

The Hessians were good religious German soldiers but what was their real purpose for fighting on the side of the British in America? The Americans were good Christian soldiers, with the purpose of fighting for freedom and our country; freedom for religion being one of those freedoms.

With our government being one of the oldest governments in the world; God has employed America many times in our history for His purposes to develop many other countries. It is so shameful to see the lowering of American principles, and the corruption in our leadership, today. The only way back to a principled and Godly country is to accept His will and purpose.

(Now the purpose of the commandment is love from a pure heart, from a good conscience and from sincere faith (NKJV 1 Tim1:5).

Holy Spirit Pray

> **Action** We understand the purpose of God, we have to do our part in making this happen. Pray, stay with Christ.

Holy Spirit

…'to open their eyes, in order to turn them from darkness to light, and from the power of Satan to God, that they may receive forgiveness of sins and an inheritance among those who are sanctified by faith in Me.'

(NKJV Acts 26:18)

Our relationship with God is monumental in our daily lives. This book is written daily thinking, talking about, and feeling this relationship with God. Jesus, and what He did for us by going to the cross, through the Holy Spirit, sanctified us and made us holy with God.

God is no longer high in the sky; He, instead, is in our heart, soul, and mind through the Spirit. He is where He has always been; in our hearts. Now, we realize this through Christ our savior; Emmanuel (Matt 1:23), which is translated "God with us." Jesus through His pain and sorrow, accomplished this for mankind.

Our job, through knowing the Trinity, is to pray for the acceptance of God's omnipotent plan, for humanity, and to help others to realize His beautiful plan.

(… 'and then to the Gentiles, that they should repent, turn to God, and do works befitting repentance' (NKJV Acts 26:20b).

Holy Spirit   Pray

> **Action**   We as Christians, should always stay with Christ, to know God's will.

Jewish People

"If I had not done among them the works which no one else did, they would have no sin; but now they have seen and also hated both Me and My Father.

(NKJV John 15:24)

The Jewish people rejected Jesus' status in the world, and most still do. They wanted a military might like David, which would have put this king above and beyond the people. The people wanted a king higher than a proletarian. They did not want to communicate with their Messiah on a personal level; even though this was God's plan (Eze 36:26) at least 700 years before Christ came.

God's will was not what they wanted; they wanted their will, their agenda. It would make them look so much more absolutistic; in the eyes of the world.

God was not enough for them; they wanted a Messiah to be an encroaching physical king, possibly to take care of the invading Romans.

This time upon Jesus' coming, they may get what they want if this is what they and the world need. God loves the Jewish people and they love Him.

("But this happened that the word might be fulfilled which is written in their law, 'They hated Me without a cause' (NKJV John 15:25).

Holy Spirit Pray

> **Action** As a human, Jesus was a Jewish Man, who was born human, lived as a human, and died as a human; He was God's Son. Stay with our beautiful and omnipotent Son of God.

Our King

"And He will reign over the house of Jacob forever, and of His kingdom there will be no end" (NKJV Luke 1:33).

As we enjoy the beautiful warm season of Christmas, we give thanks to our God for His omnipotent plan to bring humanity back in line with His principles. His wise and thoughtful plan of salvation has worked for the penniless, the well provided for, and the absurd, in a society of blistering thoughtlessness.

We are reminded each year of the intimate Christmas gift God so generously gave us; Jesus. Jesus gave us new life and rebirth by what He accomplished; our new heart and strong Spirit was predicted (Ezekiel 36:26) by God; Two thousand years of history shows Jesus is the Son of God. He showed His love for us through the cross; because of this love, He is our Savior, our God and our King for eternity.

("For with God nothing will be impossible" (NKJV Luke 1:37).

Holy Spirit   Pray

    Action   We understand we are dealing with an omnipotent God; that is why it is so important to stay with God and His will.

The Spirit of God

Now we have received, not the spirit of the world, but the Spirit who is from God, that we might know the things that have been freely given to us by God.

(NKJV 1 Corinthians 2:12)

After studying deeply and feeling the rewards of the knowledge that goes deep into the mind, a person realizes there is great satisfaction of the love that comes with knowledge. The mind can develop and grow in many different areas. It can take us into a stronger and wider path of excitement and self-sufficient entertainment of life. We can imagine a lot and can become very accomplished in our need to capture a great deal of that imagined source. This comes from our mind with all of its information and root of knowledge.

God has given us a wonderful gift; the mind. But then we feel in our soul and we use our mind to examine that feeling. We realize through our soul; we can feel the wisdom, the strength and the truth of a greater satisfaction, when touching something or someone greater than we are.

We will never qualify to dominate or control that source within our soul, but to humbly touch one little piece of it, is very gratifying. The very real satisfaction of life; to be able to respect and touch the Spirit of God.

(But God has revealed them to us through His Spirit. For the Spirit searches all things, yes, the deep things of God (NKJV 1 Cor 2:10).

Holy Spirit Pray

   Action   Humbly we ask God to stay with us.

Knowledge

O Timothy! Guard what was committed to your trust, avoiding the profane and idle babblings and contradictions of what is falsely called knowledge---

(NKJV 1 Timothy 6:20)

The well-read seems very confident in themselves because they have knowledge as their base; and words of knowledge for their lever of confidence.

The Greeks found their God through knowledge and debate, proving knowledge is good for humans to obtain. This is a very strong goal; but without the wisdom of keeping God first, the wrong path is so often taken and the wrong decisions are so often made.

God is truth and wisdom. Without the realization of the Spirit that lives within our soul as a guiding tool for Christ, we can fall into unrighteousness. Without God first, we start tolerating society and their way of thinking, rather than keeping with God and His principles.

The law of society does not supersede the law of nature. *

...by professing it, some have strayed concerning the faith. Grace be with you.

(NKJV 1 Timothy 6:21)

Holy Spirit   Pray

> **Action**   Paul was a very educated and knowledgeable man for His time; Yet, he was wise enough to know the truth of God. Stay with God.

*(Taken from Constitution Alive, David Barton and Rick Green.)

Circle of Heaven

Thick clouds cover Him, so that He cannot see, and He walks above the circle of heaven (NKJV Job 22:14).

In America, we are living in Jesus' era of moral codes or Jesus' bubble. Widows, orphans, old people are well taken care of; all the advantages of charities, Medicare, or possibly Medicaid, and the list goes on. A lot of people do not realize our country is in God's Circle of Heaven; if not from knowing Christ ourselves, then possibly from our ancestors or the founding of our country; which developed this ethical Godly right.

In any event, if we ever get a Caliphate or Communist government here in America, will we stay in God's Circle of Heaven?

Jesus is so omnipotently wholesome with an individualistic, truthful approach to all problems, there is just nothing that compares; certainly, no man-made religion or authoritarian coercive government.

In our society, Jesus does not get the credit He has earned and deserves; even though, He is still there for us every step of the way, when we ask.

("Go therefore and make disciples of all the nations.......
Teaching them to observe all things that I have commanded you" (NKJV Matthew 28:19,20)

Holy Spirit   Pray

> **Action**   Let us show our Christ how much we love and appreciate Him. Let us stay in His presence by prayer.

Spirit of Love

Now the birth of Jesus Christ was as follows: After His mother Mary was betrothed to Joseph, before they came together, she was found with child of the Holy Spirit (NKJV Matthew 1:18).

The Spirit always comes with such strength and force around this time of year. Maybe people's souls are more open and willing to share this great feeling of renewed birth and sanctification.

The assurance of Jesus' love of mankind is always an open door to the joy we feel for God's gift to humanity.

The Spirit of love is always with us through-out the year, but not with the same fortitude and mana felt at Christmas Time.

(And when they had come into the house, they saw the young Child with Mary His mother, and fell down and worshiped Him. And when they had opened their treasures, they presented gifts to Him; gold, frankincense, and myrrh.)

(NKJV Mathew 2:11)

Holy Spirit   Pray

Action   Jesus was treated with Royalty by those who knew Him personally; Just like we do when we accept Him. Stay with Him. God's gift to the world is Jesus.

Truth and Righteousness

...and with all unrighteous deception among those who perish, because they did not receive the love of the truth, that they might be saved (NKJV 2 Thess 2:10).

The importance of learning to love truth and righteousness is extremely, relevant for a young adult. Learning to love God, and what Jesus Christ suffered for humanity, is a very valued lesson.

The people, who are called by Christ, become aware of some of the main principles of God; to embellish the relationship.

As Followers of Christ, with an intimate relationship with Jesus and the Spirit, truth and righteousness is not only felt, but practiced every minute of every day for many reasons; protection being one of them.

For a man that has been investigated for six long years, our previous president found these principles have kept him safe; literally.

When God calls us for a special job, He knows exactly what He is doing. It takes us a while to understand; but our omniscient God knows, it is so important to trust and obey these principles of truth and righteousness, for our God.

(...that they all may be condemned who did not believe the truth but had pleasure in unrighteousness (NKJV 2 Thessalonians 2:12).

Holy Spirit   Pray

> **Action**   The Holy Spirit is within us, giving us God's truth; we must learn to love this truth and trust it.

Listen to the Holy Spirit

"The Spirit of truth, whom the world cannot receive, because it neither sees Him nor knows Him; but you know Him, for He dwells with you and will be in you.

(NKJV John 14:17)

We realize our souls are saved by Christ. Usually, the first question in our minds and verbally, we ask, "What is God's will?"

Everything is new, everything is different; what is said, how we think, how we feel, and the questions go on and on.

Jesus went to the cross to make us perfect in God's presence, so it is logical thinking to keep our souls clean. Even though, we will never be perfect in this world, it is a good goal and one that Jesus expects from us.

First step, in God's will is through prayer and supplication; keeping our souls pure and holy under God. Jesus and the Holy Spirit will take our souls to the next step, simply by testing to the point of strong trust on both sides of the relationship. When we are ready, the Holy Spirit will reveal to us through love and understanding, just what He wants us to reach out with our levers and do.

Remember, God is our base of truth, trust, and love; and then, we reach out actively, to do His will; just like Jesus did, our leader.

("And he who loves Me will be loved by My Father, and I will love him and manifest Myself to him" (NKJV John 14:21).

Holy Spirit   Pray

> **Action**   Jesus will take care of us and He always answers our prayers of faith and supplication; stay with Christ.